VARIATIONS
COOKBOOK
FISH & SEAFOOD

Abbreviations and Quantities

1 oz	= 1 ounce = 28 grams
1 lb	= 1 pound = 16 ounces
1 cup	= approx. 5-8 ounces * (depending on density)
1 cup	= 8 fluid ounces = 250 milliliters (liquids)
2 cups	= 1 pint (liquids)
8 pints	= 4 quarts = 1 gallon (liquids)
1 g	= 1 gram = $^1/_{1000}$ kilogram
1 kg	= 1 kilogram = 1000 grams = $2^1/_4$ lb
1 l	= 1 liter = 1000 milliliters (ml) = approx. 34 fluid ounces
125 milliliters (ml)	= approx. 8 tablespoons = $^1/_2$ cup
1 tbsp	= 1 level tablespoon = 15-20 g * (depending on density); = 15 milliliters (liquids)
1 tsp	= 1 level teaspoon = 3-5 g * (depending on density) = 5 ml (liquids)

*The weight of dry ingredients varies significantly depending on the density factor, e.g. 1 cup flour weighs less than 1 cup butter. Quantities in ingredients have been rounded up or down for convenience, where appropriate. Metric conversions may therefore not correspond exactly. It is important to use either American or metric measurements within a recipe.

British Cookery Terms

US	UK	US	UK
arugula	rocket (rocket salad)	molasses	treacle
bacon slices	streaky bacon, streaky rashers	offal	variety meats
beet	beetroot	papaya	pawpaw
bouillon cube	stock cube	parsley root	Hamburg parsley
broil, broiler	grill, oven grill	peanut, peanut oil	groundnut, groundnut oil
chicory	endive	pit	stone (of fruits)
cilantro	fresh coriander leaves	porcini mushrooms	ceps, boletus or penny bun
coconut, shredded or grated	desiccated coconut	powdered sugar	icing sugar
cookie	biscuit (sweet)	rise	prove
corn	maize, sweetcorn	rutabaga	Swede
cornstarch	cornflour	seed	pip
eggplant	aubergine	shrimp	prawn
flour, all-purpose	plain flour	slivered almonds	flaked almonds
French fries	chips	snow peas, sugar peas	mangetout
golden raisins	sultanas	Swiss chard	chard
grill	barbecue	tart	flan
ground beef or pork	minced meat or mince	tofu	beancurd
ham (cured)	gammon	tomato paste	tomato puree
heavy (whipping) cream	double cream	whole wheat	wholemeal
jelly	jam	zucchini	courgette

© h.f.ullmann publishing GmbH
Original title: *Variationenkochbuch. Fisch & Meeresfrüchte*
ISBN of the original edition: 978-3-8331-5867-4

Design, photography, layout, and typesetting: TLC Digitales Fotostudio GmbH & Co KG, Velen-Ramsdorf
Editors: Bettina Snowdon, Sylvia Winnewisser
Copy editing: Annerose Sieck

© for this English edition:
h.f.ullmann publishing GmbH

Translation from German: Rae Walter in association with First Edition Translations Ltd, Cambridge, UK
Editing: Sally Heavens in association with First Edition Translations Ltd, Cambridge, UK
Typesetting: Rob Partington in association with First Edition Translations Ltd, Cambridge, UK
Cover design: Hubert Hepfinger
Overall responsibility for production: h.f.ullmann publishing GmbH, Potsdam, Germany

ISBN 978-3-8480-0010-4

Printed in China

10 9 8 7 6 5 4 3 2 1
X IX VIII VII VI V IV III II I

www.ullmann-publishing.com
newsletter@ullmann-publishing.com

VARIATIONS
COOKBOOK

FISH & SEAFOOD

More than 200 basic recipes and variations

h.f.ullmann

CONTENTS

INTRODUCTION

Fish and seafood are a delicious and healthy part of our daily diet. This book shows you step by step how to prepare the classic dishes and gives many possible variations. Numerous suggestions for sauces and side dishes offer additional inspiration.

Before you start, take a moment to read the Introduction. Here you will find out about buying fish and gain some practical tips on processing and preparation.

Have fun experimenting—and enjoy your meals!

ABOUT THIS BOOK

Why buy this book?

You want to serve fish, because fish is healthy. Why not? But which fish? You stand in front of the fresh fish or frozen fish counter looking at cod, rockfish, salmon, mackerel, trout, tuna, or shrimp. It is difficult to decide. But when you have finally returned home from shopping, you wonder about the best way to prepare the fish or shrimp in order to bring out its full flavor. Is it better to boil, steam, fry, or grill? How long does a fish steak take to fry and still remain nice and juicy? And which spices and sauces go best with trout "au bleu"?

Your own repertoire is often limited—especially if you need to serve something different from that which you usually cook. That is when a good cookbook is worth its weight in gold. Most cookbooks offer, at most, one or two methods of preparation and no more than

one for side dishes, salads, and sauces—too few for experimenting with something new.

Advantages

This cookbook is different. It carries on from where other cookbooks stop—with the variations.

This means that you will find, not just one recipe for, say, cooking fish fillets, but at least four variations. In addition, there is a fantastic selection of side dishes, such as potatoes,

pasta, rice, and vegetables, which you can experiment with as much as you like, according to your taste. What is more, for sauce-lovers we also recommend unusual sauces and dips for almost all our dishes, as well as the classic sauces that complement them. In addition, you will find valuable hints and information about individual ingredients.

Looked at this way, this book is like a set of building blocks for innovative cooks.

How to use it

This is how it looks. The book is divided into three chapters, divided by habitat for fresh and saltwater fish, and by species for seafood.

For each dish there is a basic—usually classic—preparation method, which you may already have wanted to learn about in detail. You have the opportunity to do that here, with the step by step instructions and photos. On these pages, you will also find either information about the fish or one of the ingredients, or a recipe for a side dish or a sauce.

The following double page spread shows between four and six possible

variations on the basic recipe, each one with a helpful photo. As a little extra, we offer you either more accompaniments, such as potatoes, rice, pasta, polenta, or vegetables, or delicious sauces and dips, which you can use individually or vary as you fancy. The recipes have been assembled to suit all tastes, and from all parts of the world.

So, armed with this book, you can now surprise your family, friends, and neighbors with a dish they will not be offered every day.

We wish you every success with your cooking!

Quality

When buying fish, try to ensure they are from sustainable sources or reputable fish farms.

Farmed fish are kept exclusively for consumption, in order to put a stop to over-fishing, to maintain fish and seafood stocks, and to protect the wild fish population. Sustainable

fishing means that the stocks and reproduction of fish species are protected.

In organic fish farms, where the stocking density must be lower, the diet of the fish is also carefully controlled.

Variations

In this book, we want to present you with the best variations on every preparation method for the range of fish and seafood included, so that you have the widest possible choice of recipes. Consequently, we take different approaches according to the individual themes. For example, because a fish steak tastes best plain,

in the variations you can simply choose from the different suggested garnishes, which will complement the fried fish steak without radically altering it.

It is different with, say, fish fillets. In this case, there are many possible ways of preparing them, so there you will find versions with delicious sauces, vegetables, and dips. You will soon get to understand the principle.

As we see it, some variations can only be combined with particular side dishes, sauces, and dips. We will point this out, but here, too, you are free to experiment with new taste experiences.

Hints and tips

You do not need any special training to cook our recipes—you just need to enjoy cooking and have a kitchen with the usual equipment. Thanks to the clear descriptions and step by step instructions, our recipes can be cooked by beginners without any problems, and the variations will give even experienced cooks fresh inspiration.

Where there is something that requires particular attention, whether it is about cooking fish or preparing vegetables, we will point it out, so that nothing should go wrong.

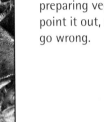

INFO
MSC SEAL OF APPROVAL

The Marine Stewardship Council (MSC) is an independent charitable organization, whose purpose is to protect fish and seafood stock from over-fishing. The MSC Seal is only awarded to products that protect endangered fish stocks and their ecosystem. Please look at the pack-aging of frozen fish to see if it bears the MSC label, and ask for it when buying from the fresh fish counter.

WHAT YOU SHOULD KNOW ABOUT FISH

Freshwater fish

Freshwater fish describes all the species of fish that live in rivers, streams, lakes, and fresh water lagoons. Some species, such as eels and salmon, spend part of their lives in both fresh and salt water.

The best known freshwater fish is probably the trout, which is a member of the salmon family.

It can be poached or fried.

Carp are found in rivers and lakes. Young carp weighing 2–4$\frac{1}{2}$ lb/1–2 kg have the best flavor. They are usually served "au bleu" (i.e. very rare). Pike live in lakes and rivers with calm, clear water. The flesh of small pike has an aromatic flavor and is lean. Pike may be stuffed, fried, or made into balls. The flesh of the pike perch, which lives in big rivers, is firm, has very few bones, and has a delicate flavor all its own. It can be cooked in all the various ways.

Salmon migrate from rivers to the sea and return to fresh water to spawn. Their flesh is rich and very aromatic. Salmon tastes good prepared in all the various ways. Perch is a popular fish with firm, tasty flesh. It is eaten grilled and fried.

Saltwater fish

Herrings are available fresh, or smoked, in aspic, and as rollmops. Fresh herrings can be fried, baked, or grilled. Mackerel, which is oilier, is nice when stuffed, grilled, fried, or smoked. Cod is air-dried to produce stockfish and the deliciously smoked klipfish. It is distinguished by lean flesh, which can be poached or fried. Rockfish fillets may be shallow-fried, baked, or deep-fried.

The monkfish, with its firm, lean flesh, tastes good fried, steamed, and even very rare. Dolphinfish, or dorado, is perfect when stuffed, but

also fried, grilled, or in salt dough. Tuna is reminiscent of veal. Tuna steaks may be grilled or fried, and tuna is often eaten rare as carpaccio or in sushi. Halibut may be fried, steamed, or grilled.

The turbot is a large flatfish, and its poached flesh is a real delicacy. Sole is white, lean, and almost boneless, and tastes good baked, fried, and poached in rolls. Plaice have very tasty flesh, which is at its best in May and June.

Seafood

Blue mussels are the best known variety. Their flesh is very tasty. Small clams have light brown shells with a dark pattern. In Italy, their flesh is much appreciated in "spaghetti alle vongole." Scallops have firm, white flesh with a sweetish flavor. The orange-colored roe sac, known as coral, is much prized by gourmets.

Small, grayish-red shrimp are found in shrimp cocktail. Small lobsters, sometimes referred to as prawns, are cooked in their shells, grilled, or added to paella. They, like their freshwater lookalike, the crayfish, have very tasty flesh. Crayfish are mostly boiled or grilled, and just served with a dip.

Squid and cuttlefish have their tentacles attached to their heads. The tubes (i.e. bodies) of small squid

are delicious when stuffed and cooked. Larger squid are cut into rings and fried, baked, or deep-fried.

Preparation

In order to be able to show you more recipes, we have omitted certain stages in the preparation from the instructions for reasons of space. These are given here and apply to all the recipes.

Wash fish thoroughly before cooking and pat dry with paper towels.

Allow frozen fish to thaw and pat dry. Onions and garlic are peeled before cooking, unless otherwise indicated. Carrots are peeled or scrubbed. Peel and pit avocados and mangoes; peel pineapple. Clean mushrooms, brush away any remaining soil, and wipe with a

damp cloth (do not wash mushrooms, as they soak up a lot of water). Use untreated citrus fruits, preferably organically grown. If you are using vegetables in their skins, always wash them, preferably in warm water. Lettuce should always be washed, preferably before tearing it into pieces, otherwise too many nutrients are lost. The water in which vegetables are cooked can be used again, if they are organic vegetables.

Kitchen equipment

As already mentioned, you do not need any special equipment for these recipes.

You should have access to a normal stove top, either gas or electric, or a ceramic or induction hob.

For baking and roasting, you need an oven.

You can grill or gratinate under the broiler in your oven. For "true" grilling, a barbecue (charcoal, hardwood, gas, or electric) is of course best. But a stove-top grill will also give the fish the typical "grill stripes."

In addition, appliances such as food processors, blenders, and handheld electric blenders are very helpful for soups, sauces, and purées.

A mill is also handy, for grinding fish, meat, potatoes, and vegetables.

More unusual kitchen appliances that are helpful, but not essential, are, for instance, a special table broiler for browning off dishes just prior to serving. Then there are steamers for cooking very delicate foods without fat, and electric slow cookers or crock pots, which make it possible to cook very slowly at low temperatures.

Kitchen utensils

To prepare the dishes in this book you need pans and skillets, at least 1 small, 1 medium, and 1 large casserole, and 1 ovenproof dish.

In addition, you will need a pan or deep-fat frier that can hold fish fillets to serve four people.

You should have 1–2 heavy, preferably cast iron or aluminum, pans with a non-stick coating. For grilling fish, it is good to have a wire grill rack.

For straining and draining, you need a sieve and a colander. A salad spinner is very useful for drying washed lettuce and other salad vegetables.

Sharp knives are indispensable: big ones for chopping fish and vegetables, smaller ones for slicing and chopping fruit, tomatoes, etc. In addition, you will need a swivel-bladed peeler for fruit and vegetables, an apple corer, a serrated knife for onions and herbs, and, ideally, a mandoline for slicing vegetables thinly and making julienne carrots, etc. A grater for vegetables and cheese is fundamental, while a nutmeg grater is also very useful. To protect your worktop, you should have 1 or 2 chopping boards, either wood or plastic.

Other useful kitchen aids are a potato masher, pasta roller, skimming spoon, wooden spoon, barbecue set, whisk, measuring jug, metal and plastic bowls—and, last but not least, kitchen scales.

COOKING METHODS

Shallow and deep-fat frying

Frying is cooking whole fish or fish fillets in fat. They can be fried in a skillet on the hob, but also in the oven. Fish fillets or steaks are good for pan-frying. Fresh tuna only requires a very short cooking time, so that the flesh remains pink and juicy inside.

The procedure: wash the fish portions or whole fish, pat thoroughly dry, and season with salt and pepper. Dust them with flour and fry, or toss in a coating of beaten egg and breadcrumbs. Children love fish fingers in a crumb coating.

Deep-fried fish are equally delicious. Small, whole, deep-fried sardines taste wonderful. Peeled shrimp, squid rings, and pieces of fish dipped in batter and deep fried in

hot oil are very popular, and well-known in England in the combination of fish and chips.

The procedure: gut the whole fish (or ask the fishmonger to do it for you.) Wash, pat dry, and rub well with salt.

Dip pieces of fish or shrimp in a batter of flour, water, and salt. Deep fry in hot fat (350 °F/180 °C) until crisp. Drain on paper towels.

Boiling

Crustaceans and shellfish such as lobster, crayfish, crabs, and mussels

are cooked alive in boiling water or stock.

The procedure: drop lobster, crayfish, and crabs head first into boiling water. The shells turn red when the flesh is cooked.

Mussels are cooked in stock or wine until the shells open. Be careful. Mussels that are not open after cooking are bad, and must not be eaten.

Au bleu

This method of preparation only applies to freshwater fish such as trout, carp, catfish, and eel.

Either a boiling stock composed of vinegar and water is poured over them, or they are simmered in this stock with vegetables and seasonings.

Steaming

Steaming is the gentlest and healthiest way of preparing fish. The fish cooks without fat in a steamer or a pressure cooker, just in the water vapor. Whole fish or fillets can be cooked in this way.

Poaching

Fish becomes deliciously tender when poached in a liquid such as stock, water, or wine. Whole fish or fillets can be cooked in this way.

They can be cooked in the oven or in a pan on the hob. Fish can be cooked on a bed of vegetables. Stuffed squid are also prepared in this way.

The procedure: put the fish in a casserole with a little fat, seasoning, and a small amount of liquid, bring to a boil, cover, transfer to the oven, and bake at about 200 °F/100 °C.

As fish fillets only need a short time to cook, you can let them simmer gently or poach in a little liquid. Single pieces can also cook directly in the sauce. Fish fillets and steaks are suitable for poaching.

Gratinating

Gratinating is all about giving cooked dishes such as fried or baked fish fillets, fish steaks, half lobsters and crayfish or mussels a crispy

crust. This may consist of cheese or a mixture of butter, spices, and nuts. You can gratinate in the oven or under the broiler.

The procedure: spread your desired mixture (cheese, herbs, nuts, seasoning, and/or breadcrumbs) over the fish fillets or seafood and bake or broil until the

cheese has melted and crust is golden brown.

Grilling

When grilling or barbecuing, the fish is cooked on the grill, on foil or on a rack. In summer, you can have the barbecue at the ready, while at other times there is the broiler in your oven.

If you do not fancy that, the fish can be cooked in a stove-top grill pan. It needs no fat and gives the fish the typical "grill stripes." The taste, however, is not quite the same as that of "proper" grilled food cooked over charcoal or hardwood.

For grilling whole fish, you can also get fish baskets, which make the process easier and guarantee that the fish will not fall apart.

For grilling, whole fish such as trout, pike perch, sardines, mackerel, and dolphinfish or dorado are best. Salmon, halibut, and tuna steaks are also good for grilling.

Shellfish should always be grilled in their shells. They can also be cooked in water beforehand, and grilled to give them that typical smoky flavor.

The procedure: before grilling, brush fish steaks well with marinade or oil, so that they do not dry out. Place them on the barbecue or under the broiler and cook for the time indicated in the recipe. Brush several times with marinade or oil during cooking, and take care that they do not char.

INFO QUANTITIES

In this book you will find that the ingredients are always given in Imperial (American) measurements followed by the Metric equivalent. Please see page 2 for a conversion table and an explanation of the abbreviations.

Sauces and Dips

With many of the dishes and their variations, we make recommendations for sauces and dips. As we restrict ourselves here to listing the ingredients without quantities, you need a little bit of experience in the kitchen.

Sauces can be made in various ways. If you are frying fish, the juices can be reserved and mixed with water, bouillon, or wine to make a sauce. With marinated fish, the marinade is poured over during cooking. This can also be used to prepare a sauce.

The sauce can be enhanced by adding light or heavy cream, sour cream, yogurt, crème fraîche, or whipping cream. It can also be given a fresh taste by adding chopped herbs, or a piquant flavor with spices.

With boiled or steamed fish, it is a good idea to also make a sauce: for instance, a horseradish or mustard sauce. In this case, the basis is usually a pale roux made by stirring flour into melted butter, then adding water, wine, or bouillon, and lastly

stirring in the actual flavoring—mustard, horseradish, or lemon juice, for example.

If you choose a cooking method where no juice runs out, such as grilling or frying, and you still want to serve a sauce with the fish, preparing a dip can be recommended. What matters is how you enhance the dip in an individual way—perhaps with onions, stewed vegetables, mushrooms, cheese, and so on.

There are also several possible ways to thicken sauces.

The classic way is with cornstarch, dissolved in a little water and stirred into the sauce, thickening it as it comes to a boil.

Sauces can be thickened with flour and butter. Rub together equal quantities of flour and cold butter, and add piece by piece to the boiling sauce.

If pieces of vegetable, potato, or fruit are being cooked in the sauce, these are puréed after cooking to make the sauce creamy.

It takes a little longer to reduce a sauce. This gives it the best taste, as the flavors of the ingredients become more intense during reduction. Tomato sauce that is reduced again after a few hours of cooking has a particularly intense flavor.

Reduced sauces can be made smooth and creamy with ice-cold butter flakes. Stir the butter into the sauce with a handheld blender and serve immediately, before the butter and sauce separate again.

When thickening with egg yolk, the egg is beaten smooth in a little milk and cream, and then slowly stirred into the hot sauce. It is important that the sauce does not boil, otherwise the egg yolk will coagulate.

When choosing the ingredients for a sauce, your imagination should know no bounds. Even unusual sauce ingredients have their attractions. In the right quantities, they will give your sauce that extra kick.

Dips taste good with grilled, fried, or deep-fried fish and seafood. As well as ready-made dips such as sauce tartare or rémoulade, which you can also make yourself, there are other delicious dips that are quick and easy to make.

When making mayonnaise for a dip, please take care to add the oil in a thin stream. And care must also be taken around lemon juice, as this can cause mayonnaise to curdle very quickly.

Side dishes

In our selection of side dishes, we have tried to strike a balance. It includes recommendations for all kinds of potato dishes, from mash, through rösti, to au gratin, as well as many rice and pasta variations—some with vegetables, some with herbs and spices, and some with fruit. It also includes grain-based side dishes, such as polenta, bulgur, and couscous.

Here, too, we have left out the quantities, as our accompaniments are only intended as suggestions for you.

Where we think that none of these filling side dishes tastes right, you will find a bread recipe, or a dish with croutons.

Other side dishes, of course, include all kinds of vegetables—fresh and frozen, stewed, steamed, boiled, gratinated, raw in salads, fresh or dried, and mixtures of two things, such as vegetables and fruit. Here, too, you can follow your own taste.

Herbs and spices

Herbs and spices are the finishing touch to every dish. They emphasize or complement the taste of vegetables, meat, and fish with their own specific aroma, while also being good for your health—many of them aid digestion.

The motto is: the fresher the better. Favorite herbs in the kitchen are parsley, chives, dill, fennel, chervil, tarragon, lovage, marjoram, thyme, oregano, sage, cilantro, and basil. They are present as ingredients in almost all the recipes. Fresh herbs are finely chopped, with the leaves usually being removed first from their hard stems or stalks. Only chives can be chopped straight away. Of course, you can also use dried herbs.

Spices and seasonings can be bought ready ground, but quite often they lose some of their flavor as a result. So, if possible, you should use freshly ground salt and pepper, and grate your own nutmeg.

One tip, however: for potatoes, assume about 1³/₄ lb–2¹/₄ lb (800 g–1 kg), for pasta around 14 oz (400 g), and for rice, corn, bulgur, and couscous, around 1¹/₄ cups (250 g) for four people. Then, you can experiment, as to whether you prefer adding 1 or 2 onions, 2 or 3 bell peppers, or 3¹/₂ oz (100 g) or 5¹/₂ oz (150 g) mushrooms to your rice, couscous, or bulgur, and enrich your polenta with 5 or 7 tablespoons of grated Parmesan.

FRESHWATER FISH

Trout, carp, pike, salmon, pike perch, and perch are popular food fish found in rivers and lakes.

These fish can be prepared in a wide variety of different ways.

They can be baked, fried, poached, or stuffed, served in a sauce, on a bed of vegetables, or in a delicious crust.

This book is filled with countless suggestions, including suitable side dishes, dips and sauces.

TROUT MEUNIÈRE
with potatoes

Serves 4

1³/₄ lb (750 g)	*potatoes*
4	*brown trout (each 9–12 oz/250–350 g), ready to cook*
	Salt
	Pepper
4 tbsp	*all-purpose flour*
7 tbsp (100 g)	*butter*
4 tbsp	*parsley, chopped*
2	*lemons, sliced*

INFO

Trout meunière: The name of this classic recipe—meunière = miller's wife or daughter—refers to the use of flour, which gives the dish its particular flavor. The coating of flour adds carbohydrates to this protein-rich fish, causing a specific reaction during frying that produces more aromatic fats and crispier surfaces than if the fish was in direct contact with the pan. In addition, the flour binds some of the fat, which also absorbs and retains flavors.

Step by step

Cook the potatoes in a little water, then peel and keep warm.

Wash the trout thoroughly, pat dry, season inside and out with salt and pepper, and toss in the flour.

In a skillet, heat 4 tablespoons of butter until it begins to foam.

Fry the trout on both sides over medium heat for 10 minutes and keep warm.

Melt the remaining butter in the skillet and briefly fry the parsley and potatoes.

Serve the trout with slices of lemon and the potato and parsley mixture.

INFO

Savoy cabbage can be used even when it has not formed a firm, tightly closed head. It is much more versatile than other kinds of cabbage, because its leaves are more delicate; on the other hand, it does not keep as long as red or white cabbage. All the same, its frost resistance gives it a certain advantage over other types of cabbage, making it an excellent winter vegetable.

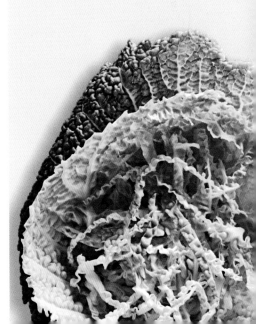

Side dish

Absolutely delicious: **creamed savoy cabbage au gratin**. Cut 1¹/₄ lb (600 g) savoy cabbage into strips and thinly slice 9 oz (250 g) mushrooms. Lightly brown 1 shallot in butter, add the mushrooms and cabbage, season with salt and pepper, pour over ²/₃ cup (150 ml) vegetable bouillon, and simmer for 10 minutes. Then mix 2 eggs with ²/₃ cup (150 ml) light cream and 5 oz (150 g) grated Emmental, and season with salt, pepper, and nutmeg. Transfer the cabbage and mushrooms to an ovenproof dish, pour over the cream mixture, and bake for about 20 minutes at 350 °F/180 °C.

SAUCES
for trout

If you want to serve more than just melted butter with your trout, why not try these variations with wine or herbs. They go well with simple fried trout and with some of the variations.

Mushroom, herb, and cream sauce

Sauté finely-chopped mushrooms in butter, add Riesling, and reduce a little. Add finely chopped herbs, light cream, and crème fraîche. Season with salt, pepper, and lemon juice. Goes well with the Gouda, herbs, ham and olives, and lemon marinade recipe variations.

Herb, white wine, and butter sauce

Heat butter briefly, and skim off the foam. Using a whisk, stir in chopped herbs such as parsley, chives, basil, and thyme, together with white wine. Goes well with the fried trout with Gouda, herbs, ham and olives, and lemon marinade recipes.

Shallot and white wine sauce

Add white wine to the pan juices from the trout. Add diced shallots and finely chopped parsley. Add light cream, heat until the sauce thickens, and season with salt and pepper. Goes well with the fried trout with herbs, ham and olives, and lemon marinade recipes.

... with a Gouda coating and almond butter

Mix 2 tablespoons flour with 1 teaspoon ground paprika and 2 tablespoons grated Gouda. Toss the trout in this mixture and sprinkle some inside. Fry in 7 tablespoons (100 g) butter over medium heat for 5–8 minutes on each side. Remove from the pan and keep warm. Lightly brown 4 tablespoons flaked almonds in the butter remaining in the skillet, and sprinkle over the trout.

... with Serrano ham and green olives

Season the trout with salt and pepper. Stuff each fish with 1 slice Serrano ham (or Parma ham if unavailable), 4 sliced, pitted green olives, and 1 tablespoon finely chopped rosemary, and secure with toothpicks. Toss the trout in a little flour and fry in 2 tablespoons olive oil for about 5 minutes on each side, until golden brown.

FRIED TROUT
several variations

Fried trout—with or without a coating—is delicious just with butter. But if stuffed as well, it tastes just as good, if not better.

... stuffed with bolete and white wine

Sauté 14 oz (400 g) bolete and season with salt and pepper. Sauté ¹/₂ bunch chopped parsley and 1 crushed garlic clove. Salt the fish, stuff with sautéed parsley and garlic, close, and coat with flour. Fry in a skillet. Spread the mushroom mixture on top and add generous ³/₄ cup (200 ml) white wine. Bake in the oven for 20 minutes.

... stuffed with herbs

Mix together the leaves of ¹/₂ bunch basil cut in strips, the leaves of ¹/₂ bunch thyme, and ¹/₂ bunch chopped parsley with 2 crushed garlic cloves, 2 diced shallots, and 2 tbsp olive oil, and season with salt and pepper. Rub and stuff the trout with the mixture, and fasten with toothpicks. Toss in flour and fry in butter, turning frequently.

... in a cornstarch coating with garlic sauce

Mix together 4 crushed garlic cloves with 1 teaspoon each vegetable bouillon granules, herbes de Provence, and the juice of ¹/₂ lemon. Pour over 7 tablespoons (100 ml) boiling water and allow to cool. Rub the trout with salt and pepper, leave to stand, wipe, and salt again. Toss in 14 oz (400 g) cornstarch, and rub it inside. Fry for 5 minutes on each side in plenty of oil until crisp.

... in a lemon and parsley marinade

Rub the trout with the juice of 1 lemon. Beat together 1 tablespoon evaporated milk and 1 egg. Mix in 2 crushed garlic cloves, salt, pepper, and ¹/₂ bunch finely chopped parsley. Brush the trout inside and out with the mixture and marinate for 1 hour. Then fry in 2 tablespoons olive oil for about 5 minutes each side, until golden brown.

TROUT "AU BLEU"
with carrots and celery

Serves 4

4	*rainbow trout (each 9–12 oz/250–350 g), ready to cook*
1	*carrot, roughly diced*
1	*celeriac, roughly diced*
1	*onion, roughly diced*
1 bunch	*parsley*
2 tsp	*peppercorns*
2	*bay leaves*
	Salt
2 cups (500 ml)	*white wine*
2 cups (500 ml)	*white wine vinegar*
1	*unwaxed lemon*
5 tbsp	*butter*

Step by step

Wash the trout thoroughly in running water, taking care not to rub off the skin.

Add the fish to the hot, but no longer boiling, vegetable stock and steep for 8–10 minutes.

Add the carrot, celeriac, onion, parsley, peppercorns, bay leaf, and salt to 10 cups (2.5 l) water and wine, bring to a boil, and leave to simmer.

Slice the lemon and arrange on the fish.

Tie the trout head to tail, from the tail fin to the gills. Heat the white wine vinegar and pour over the trout.

Melt the butter in a pan and serve separately with the trout.

WHITE WINE INFO

Unlike red wine, **white wine** is not made from must containing crushed grapes with their skins and stalks, but from the pure juice of pressed white or red grapes. As a result, it remains

light in color, ranging from pale green through golden yellow to almost brown. It also contains less tannin and histamine and is easier for sensitive people to digest. But even if you "only use it for cooking," do not use cheap, poor quality white wine, because it has a perceptibly negative effect on the taste. The rule is— use the same wine for cooking that you will be serving with the meal.

CELERIAC INFO

The part of **celeriac**—also known as celery root—used in cooking is the round tuber that grows half underground. It is used for soups, or for roasting, or as a root

vegetable in stews and casseroles, and in purées and salads (for example, Waldorf salad). Fried slices of celeriac "Schnitzel" make a tasty snack.

TROUT
v a r i o u s l y   p o a c h e d

If you do not fancy whole, "blue" trout, no problem! Use fillets instead and poach them in one of the broths or sauces suggested here—flavored with white wine, ginger, herbs, nuts, or shrimp.

... in Riesling and mushroom stock

Slice 3 carrots and 3 parsley roots and simmer for 15 minutes in salt water together with ¹/₂ onion stuck with cloves and a bay leaf. Add 1 bunch scallions, finely chopped, and 9 oz (250 g) mushrooms cut in quarters. Then add 1¹/₃ cups (330 ml) Riesling and 2 tablespoons white wine vinegar, and poach the trout fillets in the stock for 10 minutes.

... in ginger and soy sauce

Place the trout fillets in an ovenproof dish and cover with 3 crushed garlic cloves, 4 scallions cut in rounds, and slices of ginger. Drizzle with 2 tablespoons soy sauce. Arrange 4 onions cut in rings and 12 cherry tomatoes around the fish, season with salt and pepper, and sprinkle with water. Cover the dish with aluminum foil and poach for 1 hour at 340 °F/175 °C, then for a further 30 minutes at 265 °F/135 °C.

... with nuts and bell pepper in orange stock

Rub trout fillets with lime juice, salt, and pepper. Sweat 1 red and 1 green finely chopped bell pepper, ¹/₂ finely chopped red onion, 1 teaspoon cumin, 1 teaspoon grated orange peel, 1 tablespoon chopped cilantro, and 7 tablespoons (50 g) chopped filberts in butter. Add 5 tablespoons orange juice and pour over the fish. Wrap in aluminum foil and poach for 20 minutes at 425 °F/220 °C.

... with rosemary and garlic

Drizzle the trout with 2 tablespoons lemon juice and season with salt and pepper. Stuff the trout with 4 crushed garlic cloves, 4 sprigs rosemary, and 2 sprigs thyme. Place each trout on parchment paper, sprinkle 2 tablespoons vegetable bouillon over each, and fold the paper lightly over the trout. Poach for 20 minutes at 425 °F/220 °C.

SAUCES
for trout

The poaching liquid ensures that the trout becomes tender and juicy without the flesh disintegrating. You can serve the liquid—or some of it—as a tasty sauce with the fish or prepare an extra sauce with a complementary flavor.

... in herb stock
Put ¹/₂ bunch each chervil, parsley, and sorrel in an ovenproof dish and arrange trout fillets on top. Scatter with the same quantity of herbs, pour over 1 cup (250 ml) water, and cover with aluminum foil and a lid to ensure no steam can escape. Bring to a boil then poach over low heat for about 10 minutes. Keep the lid on until it is time to serve.

... with shrimp, dill, and cucumber
Mix together 2 bunches finely chopped dill, 2 finely chopped onions, 11 oz (300 g) shrimp, 2 diced cucumbers, and the juice of 1 lemon, and season with salt and pepper. Season trout fillets on both sides, place on aluminum foil, and fill with the mixture. Pour over 6 tablespoons olive oil. Close up the foil and cook for 20 minutes at 400 °F/200 °C.

Tarragon sauce
Reduce broth with white wine by half, add light cream, and reduce again. Stir in butter and chopped tarragon. Goes well with blue trout, trout in orange broth, in herb broth, and with shrimp and cucumber.

Grape and balsamic vinegar sauce
Fry shallots in oil until golden brown and drizzle with balsamic vinegar. Add vegetable bouillon and grapes, and simmer. Remove the grapes. Reduce the sauce, then return the grapes and season with salt and pepper. Goes well with the blue trout and herb broth recipes.

HORSERADISH INFO

Horseradish is one of the hottest flavorings we know. Eaten on its own, the root brings tears to the eyes, but in small amounts it is a perfect complement to many meat, fish, and egg dishes. If you want to add it to a dish, take care

not to cook it with the food. It is more usually served separately—for example, as horseradish cream or butter. It also combines very well with apples.

LEEKS INFO

Leeks are in season from June through August and again from September through December. They are a tasty ingredient for

soups and very versatile as a vegetable. They can be cooked in a variety of ways—blanched, boiled, steamed, baked, or marinated. Always clean the whole of a leek very carefully, as there may be soil particles caught between the leaves. Slit leeks lengthways from top to bottom, then you can pull the individual layers apart and rinse them under running water.

Serves 4

1	*carp (about 3¹/₄ lb/1.5 kg), ready to cook*
	Salt
	Pepper
3¹/₂ oz (100 g)	*horseradish, grated*
1 pack	*mixed root vegetables, chopped small*
1	*leek, cut in rings*
1	*onion, diced*
12 tbsp	*olive oil*
1 bunch	*parsley, finely chopped*

Step by step

Season the carp with salt and pepper, stuff with horseradish, and spread the remainder over the outside.

Baste the carp every 10 minutes or so with the remaining oil and the pan juices.

Mix the root vegetables, leek, and onion with 6 tablespoons olive oil, transfer to a baking sheet, and bake for about 10 minutes at 350 °F/180 °C.

After 30 minutes, spread the remaining vegetables around the fish.

Stuff the trout with half the vegetables and bake in the oven for 1 hour at 400 °F/200 °C.

Sprinkle the carp with parsley and serve with the vegetables.

CARP
with horseradish and roasted vegetables

SAUCES
for carp

Baked carp tastes even better with the right sauce. These piquant sauces can be served with some of the recipe variations.

CARP
several

When buying carp, make sure that the muddy taste these fish often develop has been washed away. The carp will then be delicious to eat and can be prepared in many ways. In these sample recipes, it is baked in

Apple and horseradish cream sauce
Peel and core the apples, cut in quarters, and cook until soft. Mix in 2 tablespoons grated horseradish. Fold in whisked light whipping cream. Goes well with the baked carp with horseradish, bacon, and mushroom stuffing recipes.

... with streaky bacon and butter flakes
Line a roasting pan with $1^3/_4$ oz (50 g) streaky bacon in strips and $1^3/_4$ oz (50 g) butter flakes. Rub the carp inside and out with salt and place in the pan. Spread $1^3/_4$ oz (50 g) streaky bacon strips and $1^3/_4$ oz (50 g) butter flakes alternately over the carp. Add 1 whole peeled onion and bake for about 1 hour at 400 °F/200 °C.

Béarnaise sauce
Bring white wine to a boil with wine vinegar, tarragon leaves, peppercorns, and diced onion. Strain, and allow the liquid to cool. Stir in egg yolks with a little salt, sugar, and meat bouillon. Add the liquid. Stir in a pan over hot water, adding melted butter a drop at a time, until the sauce thickens.

... with sage, cream, and tomatoes
Rub the carp with salt and pepper. Open out flat and place skin side up in a roasting pan. Pour over 3 tablespoons melted butter, dot the fish with 3 tablespoons flaked butter, and sprinkle with 2 diced tomatoes and 2 teaspoons dried sage. Bake at 400 °F/200 °C for about 30 minutes, basting occasionally. Remove the fish, add light cream to the pan juices, and bring briefly to a boil.

SAUCES
for carp

These two thick sauces are also good accompaniments for carp.

variations

various ways: with bacon, with mushroom stuffing and sour cream, split open and topped with a tomato mixture, or covered with a potato crust.

.. with mushroom stuffing and sour cream

Fry 1 chopped onion and 9 oz (250 g) sliced mushrooms. Soak 4 slices toast in ²/₃ cup (150 ml) milk, tear into pieces, and mix with the mushrooms. Season with salt, pepper, and chopped parsley. Stuff the fish with the mixture, season with salt and pepper, and cover with 2 tablespoons flaked butter. Bake for 1 hour at 400 °F/200 °C. Pour over generous ³/₄ cup (200 ml) sour cream and bake for a further 15 minutes at 350 °F/180 °C.

Walnut sauce

Soften cubes of white bread in a little carp stock, and add grated walnuts and crushed garlic. Stir vigorously, gradually adding olive oil, to give a creamy sauce. Season with salt and lemon juice. Goes well with the baked carp with bacon, mushroom stuffing, and potato crust recipe variations.

.. with a potato, herb, and cheese crust

Mix 1¹/₄ lb (600 g) boiled, mashed potatoes with 3¹/₂ tablespoons (50 g) butter, 2 tablespoons mixed herbs, 1 crushed garlic clove, and scant 1 cup (100 g) grated Emmental. Chill in the icebox. Season the carp with salt and pepper, and toss in all-purpose flour. Fry on both sides in 2 tablespoons butter until golden brown. Transfer to a baking sheet and spread with ¹/₂-in. (1-cm) thick layer of the chilled potato mixture. Bake for 15 minutes at 400 °F/200 °C.

Bell pepper sauce

Peel and dice bell peppers and toss in butter. Add vermouth, fish stock, and heavy cream, and reduce by half. Purée and pass through a fine sieve. Goes well with the baked carp with horseradish, bacon, mushroom stuffing, and potato crust variations.

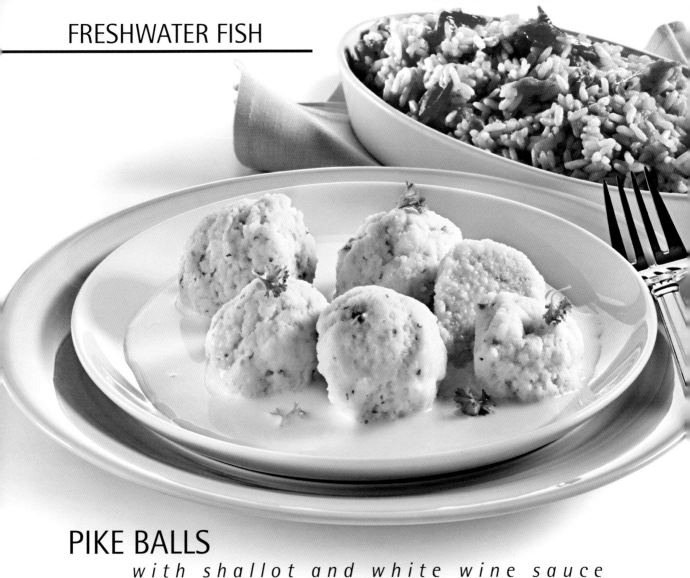

PIKE BALLS
with shallot and white wine sauce

INFO

The **tomato** is a member of the nightshade family and closely related to potatoes and tobacco. Like these, it originates from South America. Christopher Columbus brought it back to Spain from the New World in the 15th century and from there it has spread throughout the world. The red "love apple" comes in various shapes and sizes, and some have a more intense flavor than others. The small cherry or cocktail tomatoes have the strongest taste.

Serves 4

14 oz (400 g)	*pike fillets*
1	*stale bread roll, diced*
1	*egg, separated*
1¹/₄ cups (300 ml)	*light cream*
2 tbsp	*parsley, finely chopped*
	Salt
	Pepper
	Nutmeg
2	*shallots, finely chopped*
2 tbsp	*butter*
2 tsp	*cornstarch*
³/₄ cup (200 ml)	*white wine*
2¹/₂ cups (600 ml)	*fish bouillon*
4 tbsp	*Noilly Prat*

Step by step

Purée the pike fillets. Mix with the soaked and squeezed bread roll, egg white, $^2/_3$ cup (150 ml) cream, parsley, and seasoning.

Purée again until very smooth and chill in the icebox for about 1 hour.

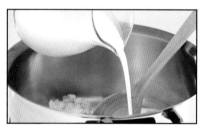

Sauté the shallots in butter until transparent. Mix the cornstarch with the wine and add to the shallots with the remaining cream. Reduce by half.

Make balls of the fish mixture, drop into the hot fish stock for about 10 minutes, remove, and keep warm.

Strain the remaining stock. Add $^3/_4$ cup (200 ml) stock and the Noilly Prat to the sauce, and reduce. Bind with the beaten egg yolk.

Salad

Lamb's lettuce can be bought ready to eat, so you no longer have the bother of washing it. Otherwise, wash it thoroughly several times, as there is often a lot of soil left in it, and cut away the roots. For the dressing, simply whisk 3 tablespoons walnut oil with 1 tablespoon balsamic vinegar, $^1/_4$ onion, very finely chopped, salt, and pepper.

Side dish

Tomato rice goes very well with this recipe. Wash 1 cup (200 g) rice. Melt 2 tablespoons butter in a pan and sauté 2 finely chopped shallots. Drain the rice, add to the shallots, and brown lightly. Add $1^2/_3$ cups (400 ml) water, salt lightly, and boil for 2 minutes without the lid. Cover and allow to swell over low heat for about 15 minutes. Mix with 11 oz (300 g) diced tomatoes.

31

SIDE DISHES
for pike balls

Rice in all forms goes well with pike balls. Here are three suggestions, varying from light to filling.

Curry rice

Sweat long-grain rice in butter until transparent. Add curry powder, pour over double the quantity of liquid (chicken bouillon is best), season with salt, and allow to swell over low heat for 20 minutes. Boil off any liquid and stir in flakes of butter.

Onion rice

Sweat long-grain rice in butter with diced onion until transparent. Add twice the quantity of water and bring to a boil. Allow to swell over low heat for 20 minutes. Before serving, break up with a fork and let the steam finish rising.

Butter rice

Sweat rice in butter with diced onion until transparent. Pour over double the quantity of bouillon and add salt. Allow to swell over low heat for 20 minutes then stir in flakes of butter.

... in tomato and mushroom sauce

For the sauce, sweat 2 finely chopped shallots until transparent and pour over 7 tablespoons (100 ml) Riesling. Add 1 crushed garlic clove, 1 bay leaf, and 5 peppercorns, pour over 1 cup (250 ml) fish bouillon, and reduce. Bring to a boil with 1 cup (250 ml) light cream. Strain. Lightly brown 7 oz (200 g) diced tomatoes and $1^3/_4$ oz (50 g) chopped mushrooms, bring to a boil in the sauce, and stir in some cream and 1 tablespoon dill.

... in watercress and potato sauce

Sauté 1 finely chopped onion in butter. Add 1 bunch finely chopped watercress. Pour over $^1/_2$ cup (125 ml) white wine and 2 cups (500 ml) bouillon. Add $5^1/_2$ oz (150 g) grated potatoes, and boil gently for about 15 minutes. Purée, season with salt, pepper, and nutmeg, and stir in $^1/_2$ cup (125 ml) light cream and 4 halved cherry tomatoes.

PIKE BALLS
s e v e r a l   v a r i a t i o n s

Here are a few suggestions for sauces to go with the basic recipe for pike balls on page 30. You can always experiment, however, and use the spices, herbs, or other ingredients that go into each sauce to make the pike balls a bit more special.

... in herb and Riesling sauce

For the sauce, simmer 1 cup (250 ml) fish stock, $^2/_3$ cup (150 ml) light cream, 4 tablespoons Riesling, and $1^1/_2$ teaspoons beurre manié for 5 minutes. Purée 1 bunch roughly chopped "green sauce" herbs (e.g. parsley, chervil, cress) with the fish sauce and 2 tablespoons butter. Season with $^1/_2$ teaspoon lemon juice, salt, and pepper.

... in lime and cream sauce

For the sauce, simmer $1^2/_3$ cups (400 ml) light cream with the juice and rind of 1 lime for 5 minutes over medium heat. Remove the pan from the heat and beat 2 egg yolks into the sauce. Season with salt and pepper.

.. in saffron sauce with prawns

Warm the pike balls in fish stock. For the final 2 minutes add generous 1 lb (500 g) peeled, cooked prawns. Heat 3 table-spoons butter, add to the pan, and add some of the stock. Fold together generous $^3/_4$ cup (200 ml) stiffly whisked light whipping cream, 3-4 saffron threads, and 2 egg yolks, stir into the sauce, and bring to a boil.

... in dill sauce

For the sauce, brown 4 tablespoons all-purpose flour in 4 table-spoons butter. Pour over 2 cups (500 ml) bouillon and season with salt and pepper. Cook for 10 minutes over low heat, stirring continuously. Thicken with 1 egg yolk. Stir in 2 tablespoons chopped dill.

SALMON RAGOUT
with cress and sour cream

Serves 4

4	slices salmon (each about 7 oz/200 g)
	Juice of ½ lemon
	Salt
1	onion, finely chopped
4 tbsp	butter
³/₄ cup (200 ml)	white wine
³/₄ cup (200 ml)	sour cream
	White pepper
1 tsp	sweet paprika
1	pack mustard cress

Step by step

Wash the salmon and pat dry with paper towels. Drizzle with a little of the lemon juice and rub with salt. Dice the flesh.

Add the white wine, cook the salmon for about 5 minutes over low heat, then remove the fish from the pan.

Sweat the onion in butter in a skillet for a few minutes, until transparent.

Add the sour cream to the pan and mix with the cooking juices. Reduce by one third.

Add the diced salmon and fry briefly on all sides.

Season with salt, pepper, paprika, and lemon juice. Stir the cress into the sauce. Add the salmon and warm briefly.

SALMON RAGOUT
several variations

Fish gotta swim—in delicious sauce, of course! Here is a selection—from zesty lemon through smooth to creamy. Just cut the salmon in strips or cubes and let it steep for a few minutes in the sauce. It will not be cooked.

... with lime and cream

Drizzle the salmon with the juice of 1 lime, season with salt and pepper, and cut into strips. Lightly brown 1 finely chopped shallot in 2 tablespoons butter. Pour over $1/2$ cup (125 ml) fish bouillon and reduce. Add $1/2$ cup (125 ml) light cream and reduce again. Add the salmon and lime juice to the boiling sauce, cover, remove from the heat, and leave to steep for 8–10 minutes until tender. Season the sauce.

... with carrot and horseradish

Bring the juice of 1 lemon, $3^{1}/_{4}$ cups (750 ml) water, 1 sliced carrot, 1 sliced onion, and 2 bay leaves to a boil. Let the salmon steep in the stock for 4 minutes. Remove the fish. Lightly brown 3 tablespoons all-purpose flour in butter, and pour over generous $1^{1}/_{2}$ cups (375 ml) of the strained stock. Bring to a boil with 7 tablespoons (100 ml) light cream and 2 tablespoons grated horseradish, and flavor with 2 tablespoons white wine, salt, pepper, and sugar. Add the salmon.

... with Mascarpone, honey, and orange rice

Grate the rind of 2 oranges and squeeze out the juice. Drizzle the salmon with 2–3 tablespoons juice and cut into cubes. Sweat 1 chopped shallot then stir in 9 oz (250 g) Mascarpone and 1 tablespoon mustard. Add the salmon and juice and cook for 10 minutes. Boil $3/_4$ cup (150 g) rice with 4 cardamom pods and the orange rind, add the remaining orange juice with 1 tablespoon each honey, cinnamon, and coriander, and allow to swell. Season with salt and pepper.

... with black olives and cherry tomatoes

Heat 4 cups (1 liter) fish bouillon, let the salmon steep in it for 8–12 minutes, then cut it into cubes. In a bain marie, beat 2 egg yolks, 2 tablespoons fish bouillon, salt, and a little lemon juice to a foam. Add $1/2$ cup (125 ml) olive oil while beating continuously until the sauce thickens. Add 6 halved cherry tomatoes, 8 pitted black olives, 2 tablespoons pine nuts, and finally the salmon.

SIDE DISHES
for salmon ragout

Noodles or rice? You decide! Lemon rice goes exceptionally well with recipes containing white wine and the variation with shrimp.

Ribbon noodles

Knead flour, eggs, and olive oil to a smooth dough, then set aside to rest for at least 30 minutes. Roll out to about $1/6$ in. (4 mm) thick. Cut ribbon noodles (about $5/8$ in. (1.5 cm) wide and 8 in. (20 cm) long), leave to dry for 15 minutes, and cook for a few minutes in boiling salt water until al dente.

Fried rice

Sweat $3/4$ cup (150 g) long-grain rice with finely chopped onion until transparent. Add twice the quantity of water and bring to a boil. Allow to swell over low heat for 20 minutes. Break up the rice with a fork and allow the steam to escape before serving.

Lemon rice

Cook $3/4$ cup (150 g) long-grain rice in twice the quantity of water with salt and a bay leaf, until al dente. Add finely chopped lemon balm and lemon zest.

... with Prosecco, tomatoes, and crème fraîche

Lightly fry 3 chopped shallots and 1 chopped carrot in olive oil. Add 1 tablespoon tomato purée, 1 tablespoon mustard, and 4 peeled, diced tomatoes, and cook for 5 minutes. Add generous $3/4$ cup (200 ml) Prosecco and 2 cups (500 ml) bouillon and reduce. Add the salmon, heat briefly, add $1/2$ cup (125 ml) crème fraîche, and leave the salmon to steep for 10 minutes. Season with salt, pepper, and tarragon.

... with celery and shrimp

Sweat $3^1/2$ oz (100 g) onions cut into rings, 7 oz (200 g) celery cut into batons, and 3 crushed garlic cloves in 2 tablespoons oil for 5 minutes. Add $1^1/4$ lb (600 g) leeks cut into rings and 1 teaspoon tarragon, pour over 2 cups (500 ml) bouillon, and simmer for a further 5 minutes. Add the salmon and $3^1/2$ oz (100 g) shrimp and leave to steep for 8–10 minutes over low heat. Mix in the grated rind of 1 lime and season with salt and pepper.

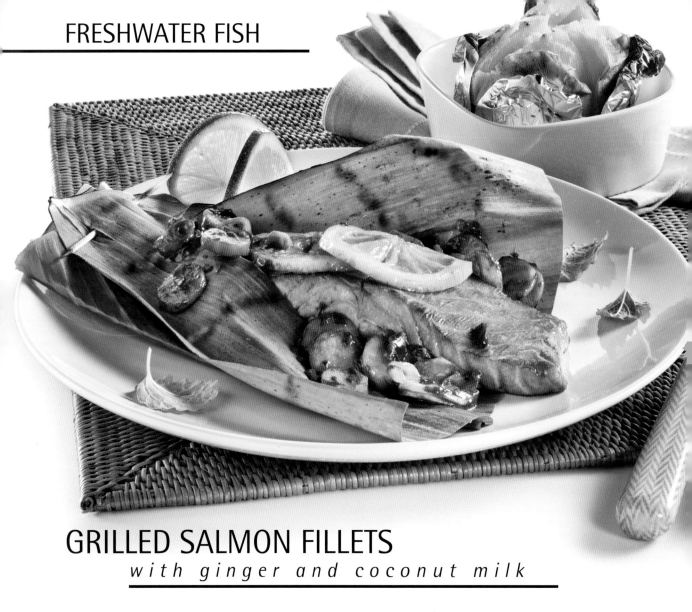

GRILLED SALMON FILLETS
with ginger and coconut milk

Serves 4

4	salmon fillets (each about 7 oz/200 g)
4 tbsp	soy sauce
1³/₄ oz (50 g)	ginger, grated
	Lime (juice of)
1	chile, deseeded and chopped
³/₄ cup (200 ml)	coconut milk
	Untreated banana leaves
3	carrots, thinly sliced
3	parsley roots, sliced
3	scallions, thinly sliced
3¹/₂ tbsp	sweet chili sauce
2	lemons, sliced
	Salt and pepper
	Chile powder

INFO

How to make your own **coconut milk**: boil 4–5¹/₂ oz (120–150 g) unsweetened, grated coconut in 1 cup (250 ml) water, milk, or coconut water (or a mixture of these) in a covered pan for 30 minutes and strain through a fine cloth. Gather the corners of the cloth together and squeeze the liquid out of the grated coconut. After a while, a creamy layer will form on the surface of the milk, which should be stirred back into the milk or removed with a spoon and used elsewhere.

Step by step

Wash the salmon fillets under cold running water and pat dry with paper towels.

Mix the soy sauce, ginger, lime juice, chile, and coconut milk, and pour evenly over the fillets. Marinate in the icebox for 6 hours.

Cut the banana leaves in pieces 8 x 12 in. (20 x 30 cm). Heat them on the grill until they shine.

Mix the vegetables with the chili sauce. Remove the salmon from the marinade and arrange 1 fillet and a quarter of the vegetables on each banana leaf.

Top each fillet with 2 lemon slices. Drizzle with a little marinade and season with salt, pepper, and chile powder.

Wrap the salmon in the banana leaves, place on a hot grill, and cook for 6–8 minutes on each side.

INFO

This method of grilling fish in **banana leaves** comes from South East Asia. The leaves keep the fish from drying out. They must first be quickly toasted to make them more flexible so they do not tear. Wrap the fish in the banana leaf, preferably with a little lemon juice and oil—or, as here, just a little marinade and whole slices of lemon. Banana leaves can be bought in Asian shops. If you cannot get hold of banana leaves, you can use several layers of foil instead.

Side dish

If you are using the grill anyway, why not make some **potatoes baked in foil** as well? For this you need to scrub 1³/₄ lb (750 g) large, preferably waxy potatoes under running water, dry thoroughly, and cut in half lengthwise. Brush aluminum foil on the inside with oil before wrapping the potatoes in it. The potatoes will take about an hour to cook through, so put them on the grill in good time! You can test to see if they are soft—careful, they are hot!—by putting a foil-wrapped potato in a towel and squeezing gently. The potato should give a little. Serve with salt and butter flakes.

DIPS
for salmon

Herbs—especially dill—are always a good complement to fish. Horseradish is also a favorite accompaniment, especially for salmon. Here you can see which dip suits which variation best.

Dill butter dip
Mix finely chopped dill with softened butter and season with lemon juice, salt, and pepper. Goes well with the grilled salmon with dill and fennel, and soy and mustard marinade recipes.

Mustard, dill, and egg dip
Mix sour cream, finely chopped hard-boiled egg, mustard seeds, mustard, dill, sugar, and a little lemon juice, and season with salt and pepper. Goes well with grilled salmon with dill and fennel and the soy and mustard marinade variations.

Herb and spinach dip
Finely chop herbs and spinach, mix with mayonnaise, and season with salt, pepper, and lemon juice. If you want fewer calories, replace the mayonnaise wholly or partly with yogurt. Goes well with grilled salmon with dill and fennel, soy and mustard marinade, and coriander and cinnamon.

GRILLED SALMON FILLETS
several

Grilled salmon is quite simply irresistible. If you want it to be especially juicy, just grill it in foil or wrapped in a banana leaf. If you particularly like a crisp skin, grill it directly on the skin side. Here are variations on grilled salmon fillet that give the fish wonderful

... with coriander and cinnamon
Briefly toast 1 tablespoon coriander seeds, crush to a fine powder in a mortar with 1 tablespoon peppercorns, and mix with $1/_2$ teaspoon cinnamon, 1 teaspoon sweet paprika, 1 pinch ground cloves, and salt. Stir in 1 bunch finely chopped dill. Rub the flesh side of the salmon fillets with the mixture. Grill the salmon with the skin side on the barbecue or for 6–8 minutes on each side under the broiler.

... with soy sauce, tomato purée, and mustard
Prepare a marinade from 1 finely chopped onion, 8 tablespoons tomato purée, 8 tablespoons olive oil, $3/_4$ cup (200 ml) soy sauce, 2 crushed garlic cloves, 3 teaspoons mustard, the juice of 1 lemon, salt, pepper, and sugar. Marinate the salmon fillets for 6 hours in the icebox. Wrap in aluminum foil and grill on both sides for 6–8 minutes.

SALADS
for salmon

Spring salads with green asparagus and sugar snap peas, or fall salads with lamb's lettuce and pears, are all perfect with salmon.

Lamb's lettuce with pears and Gorgonzola

Crumble the Gorgonzola and mix with yogurt, chopped parsley, salt, and pepper. Make a vinaigrette with balsamic vinegar, salt, pepper, mustard powder, and olive oil. Mix in lamb's lettuce, diced pears, and chopped walnuts. Top with the Gorgonzola cream.

Iceberg salad

Tear iceberg lettuce leaves in pieces and mix with drained, canned mandarin oranges. For the dressing: stir together crème fraîche, lemon juice, mandarin juice from the can, salt, and pepper, and mix with the lettuce.

Green asparagus salad

Peel the bottom third of green asparagus shoots, cut in pieces, and boil al dente. Boil the sugar snaps al dente. Make a vinaigrette with diced shallots, some of the asparagus cooking water, mustard, pepper, white wine, sherry vinegar, sunflower oil, and walnut oil. Pour over the vegetables and sprinkle with diced, hard-boiled egg.

---

variations

flavors by marinating or applying a rub to the flesh side. All the variations are suitable for grilling on charcoal, gas, or electric barbecues, and under the broiler in your oven.

... with dill, fennel, and parsley

Marinate salmon fillets for 1 hour in 7 tablespoons (100 ml) olive oil. Fry for 2 minutes on each side. divide 4 parsley sprigs, a little fennel, 1 bunch dill, and 4 bay leaves into 4 equally-sized bunches, and tie. Place each bunch of herbs on a piece of oiled aluminum foil. Lay the salmon on top and season with salt and pepper. Top with slices of lemon and grill for 6 minutes on each side.

... with white wine and lemon

Marinate salmon fillets in 7 tablespoons (100 ml) each white wine and olive oil, 1 tablespoon brown sugar, 1 tablespoon molasses, 1 tablespoon soy sauce, 1 crushed garlic clove, salt, and pepper. Grill for a total of about 10 minutes, brushing regularly with the marinade. Cut a lemon in segments and place on top of the fish about half-way through the cooking time.

SPINACH INFO

Spinach is a leaf vegetable; a member of the goosefoot family. It can be sown all year round and is called spring, summer, fall, or winter spinach, according to when it is sown.

The most delicate is young spring spinach, which can be eaten raw in salads. Summer spinach can still be used in salads, while the tougher leaves of fall and winter spinach are better blanched and eaten as a vegetable. Spinach contains many vitamins and minerals—that is what makes it so healthy.

PANCAKES INFO

The spinach and egg mixture can also be used to make thin **pancakes**. It is not necessary to pre-heat the oven for these. You

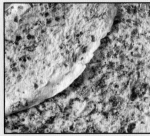

can then roll up the pancakes, or simply spread the ingredients on them and serve as an appetizer.

Serves 4

9 oz (250 g)	*frozen spinach, thawed*
4	*eggs, separated*
	Salt
	Pepper
	Nutmeg
11 oz (300 g)	*cream cheese*
1 tsp	*lemon juice*
9 oz (250 g)	*smoked salmon, sliced*

Step by step

Drain the spinach, squeeze, and chop roughly. Mix with the egg yolks and season with salt, pepper, and nutmeg.

Beat the egg whites until stiff and fold into the spinach. Line a baking sheet with parchment paper and spread the mixture over it. Bake for 15–20 minutes at 400 °F/200 °C.

Tip the baked mixture off the baking sheet, lay a sheet of parchment paper on top, and roll up the pancake with the paper.

Mix together the cream cheese, lemon juice, salt, and pepper. Unroll the pancake, remove the parchment paper, and cover the pancake with cheese mixture and slices of salmon.

Cut the sheet of pancake in half lengthwise and roll up each half. Wrap in plastic wrap and refrigerate.

Cut in ³/₈-in. (1-cm) thick slices shortly before serving.

SALMON ROLLS
with spinach pancake

SAUCES
for salmon rolls

Salmon rolls taste even better when dipped in delicious sauces, creams, and marinades. These suggestions go well with all the variations.

Sherry sauce

Heat bouillon, add sherry and light cream, and bind with cornstarch. Season with salt, pepper, and lemon juice. Beat the same quantity of light cream until stiff, mix with egg yolk and herbs, and stir into the sauce. Warm with care, and do not allow to boil!

Lime sauce

Stir sugar into yogurt until smooth. Mix lime juice with the yogurt and stir in wafer-thin strips of lime.

Fennel sauce

Sweat finely chopped shallots and pour over white wine. Toast fennel seeds in a dry pan, add sparkling wine, and reduce. Add light cream and shallots, and bring back to a boil. Strain, then season with salt, pepper, and nutmeg.

... with shrimp, bell pepper, and cream cheese

Mix 7 oz (200 g) cream cheese, $^1/_2$ red and $^1/_2$ green bell pepper, very finely diced, $3^1/_2$ oz (100 g) shrimp, 2 teaspoons lemon juice, salt, and pepper. Arrange 7 oz (200 g) sliced smoked salmon, slightly overlapping, in a rectangle on plastic wrap. Spread cream cheese over one third of the surface. Roll up and refrigerate for 4 hours. Then remove the plastic wrap and slice the roll diagonally.

... with mango and dill

Mix $4^1/_2$ oz (125 g) cream cheese with $^1/_2$ diced mango, $^1/_2$ bunch finely chopped dill, salt, pepper, lime juice, and chile powder. Arrange 7 oz (200 g) sliced smoked salmon, slightly overlapping, in a rectangle on plastic wrap. Spread with the mixture. Roll up and refrigerate for 4 hours. Then remove the plastic wrap and slice the roll diagonally.

SALMON ROLLS
several variations

These easily prepared salmon rolls make a classy appetizer and look wonderful on a cold buffet. They are perfect as finger food, especially if you spike each one with a wooden cocktail pick.

... with spinach, chives, and basil

Bake 6 spinach pancakes. Mix together 3 tablespoons chopped chives, $2^1/_2$ cups (600 g) crème fraîche, sugar, salt, cayenne, and lemon juice. Spread over the spinach pancakes, arrange 2 slices smoked salmon and 2 basil leaves on each, wrap in plastic wrap, and refrigerate for 4 hours. Remove the plastic wrap and slice the roll diagonally.

... with fennel, gherkin, and herbs

Dice $^1/_4$ fennel, $^1/_2$ red bell pepper, 1 onion, and 1 gherkin. Mix $3^1/_2$ tablespoons (50 g) crème fraîche, processed cream cheese, and chopped herbs, and season with salt and pepper. Dissolve gelatine in 2 cups (500 ml) water. Arrange 7 oz (200 g) smoked salmon on plastic wrap. Spread with the mixture. Roll up and refrigerate for 4 hours. Remove the plastic wrap and slice the roll diagonally.

... with eggs, parsley, and processed cheese

Mix 2 very finely chopped hard-boiled eggs with $^1/_2$ bunch finely chopped parsley, $4^1/_2$ oz (125 g) processed cream cheese, salt, and pepper. Arrange 7 oz (200 g) sliced smoked salmon, slightly overlapping, in a rectangle on plastic wrap. Spread with the mixture. Roll up and refrigerate for 4 hours. Then remove the plastic wrap and slice the roll diagonally.

... with cucumber, dill, and trout caviar

Arrange $^1/_2$ bunch finely chopped dill, a few strips of oak leaf lettuce, and $^1/_3$ cucumber, in strips, on each $^1/_2$ slice smoked salmon and roll up. Cut the remaining $^2/_3$ cucumber in diagonal slices, arrange the salmon rolls on top, and spread evenly with 4 tablespoons trout caviar. Garnish with lemon slices and dill before serving.

MARINADED SALMON TROUT
with mustard and dill

INFO

Marinating is steeping raw meat or fish in a spicy, often sour, liquid, called a marinade. The effect of this method is to force the spices and acids deep into the food. This gives it more flavor, while the acid makes it tender and more delicate. After marinating, meat is usually stewed, fried, or grilled, whereas fish is sometimes eaten without any further preparation (e.g. gravlax).

Serves 4

1	*salmon trout (about 2¹/₂ lbs/1.2 kg), ready to cook*
4 tbsp	*coarse salt*
4 tbsp	*sugar*
1 tsp	*white pepper, coarsely ground*
2 bunches	*dill, finely chopped*
3 tbsp	*coarse mustard*
1 tbsp	*wine vinegar*
4 tbsp	*olive oil*
	Salt
	Pepper
1	*unwaxed lemon, cut in segments*

Step by step

Wash the salmon trout, pat dry, and cut into fillets without removing the skin.

Mix coarse salt, 3 tablespoons sugar, and coarse pepper, and rub the salmon trout fillets with the mixture.

Place a fillet, skin down, in a pan, cover with half the dill, then place a second fillet on top, skin side up.

Sprinkle with half the remaining dill. Cover with aluminum foil and marinate in the icebox for 1–2 days, turning the fish several times.

Stir together the remaining sugar, mustard, vinegar, oil, salt, pepper, and dill. Slice the fish and serve with the dressing and lemon segments.

Side dishes

Noodles, rice, boiled potatoes, or puréed potatoes all go well with this—and so does **mashed potato**, which is really easy to prepare. All you have to do is boil 1³/₄ lb (750 g) mealy potatoes, let them cool a little, peel, and add salt. Then add 3 tablespoons butter, mash roughly with a potato masher—and that's it!

Salad

The hot spicy taste of **arugula** is wonderful with the mustard and dill version. Prepare a salad of arugula with a Mediterranean dressing: clean and wash 11 oz (300 g) arugula. Make a dressing with 2 tablespoons balsamic vinegar, 2 tablespoons bouillon, 8 tablespoons olive oil, salt, 2 tablespoons finely diced tomatoes, 2 tablespoons basil cut in strips, and 2 tablespoons toasted pine nuts, then pour over the salad.

47

DIPS
for salmon trout

Mustard is a good partner for salmon trout, so here are two kinds of mayonnaise with mustard. Or, if you prefer a fresher taste, try the lime cream sauce.

Mustard, honey, and dill mayonnaise
Beat egg yolk and mustard together with a whisk. While continuing to beat, gradually add oil. Stir in the honey and dill. Goes well with salmon trout with mustard and dill, orange, anise, and cloves, and lemon balm and Cognac.

Grape juice and pepper cream
Reduce red grape juice by two-thirds, stir in crème fraîche, and add peppercorns. Goes well with salmon trout with mustard and dill, orange, anise, and cloves, and lime and honey.

MARINATED SALMON
severa

Marinated salmon trout has a more refined taste than ordinary marinated salmon (gravlax), but of course you can equally well use salmon fillets. Salmon trout must remain in the marinade for 1–3 days. Bear this in mind, when you try out the recipe.

... with orange, anise, and cloves
Mix 1 teaspoon pepper, 3 cloves, $^1/_3$ oz (10 g) star anise with the grated rind of 2 lemons and 2 oranges and crush in a mortar. Mix with generous 1 lb (500 g) salt and the same quantity of sugar. Add $^1/_2$ bunch roughly chopped herbs (chervil, dill, parsley). Spread the mixture thickly over the salmon trout fillets. Cover with aluminum foil and allow to draw for 24 hours in the icebox. Rinse.

... with basil and chile
Mix 3 tablespoons cane sugar, 5 tablespoons coarse salt, 1 tablespoon coriander, and 2 finely chopped chiles, and rub the salmon trout fillets with the mixture. Put sprigs from 1 bunch basil in between. Cover and leave to draw in the refrigerator for 2–3 days. Pour off the marinade before serving.

ROUT
variations

Here you will find fresh, fruity, and lemony marinades, one with a touch of Christmas, and a hot, spicy version. Serve with one or more of the sauces on page 49. Absolutely delicious!

.. with lemon balm, peppermint, and Cognac

Crush $^1/_2$ teaspoon each black and white peppercorns, juniper berries, allspice, and coriander in a mortar. Finely chop $^1/_2$ bunch dill, $^1/_2$ bunch lemon balm, and a little peppermint, and mix all the ingredients together. Rub the fish fillets with generous $^1/_4$ cup (200 ml) Cognac. Cover with the marinade, and leave to draw in a covered bowl in the icebox for at least 24 hours. Pour off the marinade before serving.

.. with lime, cilantro, and honey

Mix the juice and grated rind of $^1/_2$ lime, 1 teaspoon crushed black pepper, 1 finely chopped chile, 1 bunch cilantro, finely chopped, tablespoons salt, 3 tablespoons sugar, 1 tablespoon olive oil, and honey to a paste. Rub into the fillets. Cover and leave to draw for days in the icebox. Wipe off the rub before serving.

SAUCES
for salmon trout

Salmon trout can be made very classy with garlic and white wine, slightly spicy with tomatoes and tarragon, or hot, slightly sour, and fruity with grape juice and pepper.

White wine sauce

Sweat shallots and crushed garlic in butter until transparent. Add diced tomatoes and pour over white wine (e.g. Muscadet). Add tarragon and reduce a little. Season with salt and pepper. Stir in crème fraîche. Goes well with salmon trout with orange, anise, and cloves, with lemon balm and Cognac, with basil and chile, and with lime and honey.

Lime cream sauce

Boil light cream with the juice and rind of a lime for 5 minutes. Remove from the heat, and beat egg yolk into the sauce. Season with salt and pepper. Goes well with salmon trout with orange, anise, and cloves, with lemon balm and Cognac, and with lime and honey.

PERCH
with a herb crust

Serves 4

1	*perch (about 2¹/₂ lb/1.2 kg), ready to cook*
	or
4	*perch fillets (each about 7 oz/200 g)*
	Salt
	Pepper
2 tbsp	*mustard*
8 tbsp	*dried breadcrumbs*
4 tbsp	*olive oil*
1 bunch	*chives, in rings*
1 bunch	*dill, finely chopped*
1 bunch	*chervil, finely chopped*
2 tbsp	*butter*

Step by step

Wash the fish under running water, pat dry with paper towels, and rub inside and out with salt and pepper.

With a spoon, spread the herb mixture evenly over the fish and dot with butter.

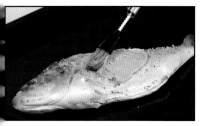

Place on a baking sheet. Spread the upper side of the perch with mustard.

Bake for about 20 minutes at 400 °F/200 °C on the middle shelf of the oven.

Mix the breadcrumbs with olive oil. Stir in the herbs, and season with salt and pepper.

If necessary, cover with aluminum foil so the fish does not get too dark.

CHIVES INFO

Chives belong to the onion family. In Germany, they have many different names, indicating a long tradition of use in the kitchen. One of the names even suggests that their antiseptic properties have long been known

as a treatment for cuts. We use raw chives for flavoring, as they lose their sharpness when cooked. Their round, purple flowers can also be used to make salads more decorative.

CHERVIL INFO

With its white umbels, meadow chervil is a common plant that most children would recognize. Its relative, the true **chervil**, is mainly used as a flavoring. It has

a delicate, ethereal, almost sweet aroma, and is mainly used in soups, salads, and sauces. It looks a bit like flat-leaved parsley, but its feathery leaves are a little finer. Chervil is a component of famous herb mixtures such as "fines herbes" or Frankfurt Green Sauce.

PERCH
several variations

For these recipes, you can of course use other species of perch, such as the rosefish or ocean perch, which is a sea fish. Baked with a crispy crust or mixed vegetables, whole or in fillets, it tastes delicious.

... with a carrot and nut crust

Mix together 1 finely grated carrot, 8 tablespoons dried breadcrumbs, scant 2 cups (150 g) ground filberts, 2 eggs, 3–4 tablespoons olive oil, salt, pepper, and 2 tablespoons chopped cilantro. Spread the mixture over the fish fillets and bake in an ovenproof dish for 20 minutes at 400 °F/200 °C.

... with a bell pepper, eggplant, and Feta crust

Sweat 2 crushed garlic cloves and 2 diced onions. Cut 1 green bell pepper in strips and add 1 diced eggplant, 1 diced zucchini, and 4 tomatoes. Add 7 tablespoons (100 ml) white wine, basil, oregano, salt, pepper, and sugar, and cook for 5 minutes. Pour over the fish fillets, cover, and bake for 10 minutes at 350 °F/180 °C. Sprinkle with $5\frac{1}{2}$ oz (150 g) Feta and bake for 10 minutes.

... with a spinach, cheese, and almond crust

Sweat 1 diced onion in 1 tablespoon olive oil together with 11 oz (300 g) fresh spinach, and season with salt and pepper. Season the fish with lemon juice, salt, and pepper, and place in an ovenproof dish. Spread the spinach mixture over the fillets. Mix together $1\frac{1}{3}$ cups (150 g) grated Emmental and 10 tablespoons (150 g) crème fraîche and spread over the spinach. Sprinkle with 2 oz (50 g) flaked almonds. Bake for 20 minutes at 400 °F/200 °C.

... with a leek and carrot crust

Sauté 1 diced onion. Add 1 leek cut in rings and 1 diced carrot and fry briefly. Pour over $\frac{1}{2}$ cup (125 ml) bouillon. Reduce the liquid almost completely. Arrange the vegetables on top of the fillets, season with dill and pepper, and spread with 1 cup (250 ml) sour cream. Leave to draw for 5 minutes, transfer to an ovenproof dish, and bake for about 20 minutes at 400 °F/ 200 °C.

SIDE DISHES
for perch

Here is a selection of three accompaniments to suit different tastes:

Tomato potatoes

Fry diced potatoes and onion in oil. Add canned tomatoes with the juice from the can. Season with salt, pepper, and basil, cover, and cook until soft. Serve with grated Parmesan.

Couscous

Bring 1$\frac{1}{4}$ cups (250 g) couscous to a boil with about two cups (500 ml) vegetable bouillon and a little salt. Leave to swell for a few minutes—and that's it!

Wild rice

Soak 1$\frac{1}{4}$ cups (250 g) wild rice for 1 hour in about 2 cups (500 ml) boiling water. Then cook without salt for 30–35 minutes over low heat. Lastly, add salt.

... with a mushroom, ham, and tomato crust

Drizzle the fillets with lemon juice. Cut 1 onion into rings and sauté. Add 3$\frac{1}{2}$ oz (100 g) sliced mushrooms and 5$\frac{1}{2}$ oz (150 g) diced ham. Finally, add the diced flesh of 5 beefsteak tomatoes and 1 bunch each finely chopped parsley and basil. Season with salt and pepper. Spread over the fish together with 9 oz (250 g) sliced mozzarella. Bake for 20 minutes at 400 °F/200 °C.

... with a mango and thyme crust

Cut the crusts from 2 slices white bread and pulse in a blender. Knead together with $\frac{1}{2}$ tablespoon thyme and 3 tablespoons butter and season with salt and pepper. Drizzle the fish fillets with lemon juice and season with salt and pepper. Fry on both sides in 1 tablespoon olive oil. Transfer to an ovenproof dish, top with 1 mango cut in strips, and then spread with the bread and butter mix. Bake for 20 minutes at 400 °F/ 200 °C.

PIKE PERCH
with mushrooms, bacon, and leeks

Serves 4

2 oz (60 g)	bacon, diced
1 tbsp	butter
1 small	zucchini, sliced
12 oz (350 g)	mushrooms, sliced
3¹/₂ oz (100 g)	leeks, cut in rounds
	Salt
	Pepper
10 tbsp (150 g)	crème fraîche
4	pike perch fillets (each 7 oz/200 g)
2 tbsp	lemon juice
2	slices white bread
1 bunch	dill, finely chopped
3 tbsp	butter, melted

INFO

The term "poach" refers to the cooking of **poached eggs**, or "oeufs pochés," as they are called in France. Eggs are poached by letting a raw egg without the shell—that is, only the yolk surrounded by the white—slide gently into hot water. The water must have a temperature of 170–200 °F/75–95 °C, and must on no account boil. This method of cooking is particularly suitable for fish, as boiling would cause the delicate flesh to fall apart.

Step by step

Fry the bacon in butter then remove from the pan. Fry the zucchini, mushrooms, and half the leeks in the same pan, season with salt and pepper, and remove.

Sauté the other half of the leeks in the same pan then stir in 6 tablespoons (100 g) crème fraîche.

Layer the fried zucchini, half the fried mushrooms, and fried leeks in an oven-proof dish.

Season the fish with salt and pepper and drizzle with lemon juice. Place the fish on top of the vegetables. Spread the leeks in crème fraîche over it and add the remaining mushrooms.

Crumble the bread and mix with two-thirds of the dill and melted butter. Spread over the fish, together with the bacon and the remaining crème fraîche.

Bake for 25 minutes at 340 °F/175 °C. Garnish with the remaining dill.

INFO

For many people, **rice** is their most important food. Altogether, there are between 8,000 and 120,000 varieties of rice in the world—the figures vary. In the trade, they draw a rough distinction between long-grain and round-grain rice (also known as pudding rice). With both long-grain and round-grain rice, there is a further distinction between varieties with transparent grains and those that are dark-grained.

Side dishes

With this fish serve only **rice**, which you can prepare in different ways. Here is a recipe for fried rice, which acquires extra flavor through the addition of an onion. Sweat 1¼ cups (250 g) long-grain rice with 1 finely chopped onion until transparent. Add 2½ cups (600 ml) water and bring to a boil. Allow to swell for 20 minutes over low heat. Before serving, break up with a fork and let the steam escape.

SAUCES
for pike perch

Served on a bed of vegetables, pike perch does not necessarily need a sauce. However, the right sauce can still bring out the flavor. Just try it!

Bell pepper and thyme sauce
Sweat diced bell pepper and shallot rings in butter until transparent, then season with ground paprika, thyme, and garlic. Simmer in fish bouillon for about 15 minutes and then strain. Goes well with all variations.

Beet sauce
Sweat onions in a mixture of butter and oil. Add beet juice and sugar, and simmer for 15 minutes. Season with salt, pepper, and raspberry vinegar. Goes well with pike perch on bacon and leek, kohlrabi and cress, sauerkraut and bell pepper, and bell pepper and fennel.

Saffron cream sauce
Lightly brown diced onion and crushed garlic in oil. Pour over lemon juice and white wine. Add bouillon, light cream, and saffron. Season with salt, pepper, and dill. Goes well with all variations.

... on zucchini and Gruyère
Sweat 2 yellow bell peppers, cut into strips, with 2 sliced zucchini, and 2 sticks celery in batons. Simmer in generous $^3/_4$ cup (200 ml) vegetable bouillon and season with salt and pepper. Transfer to an ovenproof dish and place the fish on top of the vegetables. Top with scant 1 cup (100 g) grated Gruyère, $3^1/_2$ oz (100 g) Mascarpone, 2 tablespoons white wine, 1 teaspoon curry powder, chopped chives, and thyme. Bake for 20 minutes at 400 °F/200 °C.

... on sauerkraut and green bell pepper
Fry 2 onions cut into rings and 1 green bell pepper in strips in 2 tablespoons butter. Add 14 oz (400 g) canned sauerkraut, season with salt and pepper, and simmer. Drizzle pike perch fillets with lemon juice and season with salt and pepper. Transfer the sauerkraut to an ovenproof dish and arrange the fish on top. Pour over $^1/_2$ cup (125 ml) light cream seasoned with ground paprika. Bake for 20 minutes at 400 °F/200 °C.

PIKE PERCH ON A BED OF VEGETABLES
several variations

Pike perch has particularly firm flesh with few bones, which makes it a special favorite with those who love fish. Poaching on a bed of vegetables draws wonderful flavors into the flesh.

... on potatoes and herbs

Fry 2 finely chopped onions and 1³/₄ lb (750 g) potatoes, diced small, in 3 tablespoons butter, season with salt, and pour over 2 cups (500 ml) bouillon. Add 1 finely chopped red bell pepper, a little basil, lovage, and parsley, and season with salt and pepper. Transfer to an ovenproof dish and arrange the fillets on top. Brush with 2 tablespoons melted butter. Bake for 30 minutes at 250 °F/120 °C.

... on kohlrabi and cress

Sweat 2 leeks cut into rounds. Add 2 diced potatoes and 1 diced kohlrabi, pour over ²/₃ cup (150 ml) fish bouillon, cover, and simmer. Mix 1 pack finely chopped mustard cress with 3 tablespoons butter, mix in the kohlrabi and potatoes, and season with salt, pepper, and nutmeg. Transfer to an ovenproof dish. Season the fish fillets with salt and pepper and arrange them on top. Bake for 20 minutes at 400 °F/ 200 °C.

.. on carrots and mushrooms

Mix 9 oz (250 g) sliced carrots, generous 1 lb (500 g) halved potatoes, 9 oz (250 g) halved mushrooms, 1 bunch scallions cut into rings, and 1 bunch chopped parsley in a casserole. Add 14 oz (400 g) canned tomatoes, 1 packet mixed fish spices, and pour over ¹/₂ cup (125 ml) white wine. Place the fish on top. Cover and bake for about 60 minutes at 400 °F/ 200 °C.

... with red bell pepper and fennel

Dice 1 red bell pepper and 1 fennel and spread on a baking sheet. Lay the fish fillets on top, covered with the slices of 1 lime. Scatter 3 crushed garlic cloves, leaves from 3 sprigs each rosemary and thyme, 5 cardamom pods, 1 tablespoon red pepper, 3 star anis, and ¹/₂ tablespoon salt around the fish. Pour over ²/₃ cup (150 ml) olive oil. Bake for 20 minutes at 400 °F/200 °C.

SALTWATER FISH

The sea contains many fish that are delicious to eat.

From herring—from which we get Matjes fillets—cod, ocean perch/ rosefish, and tuna through special delicacies like turbot and sole.

Crisply fried or delicately simmered—there are many ways of preparing them.

In this section you will find, not only lots of fish recipes, but also accompaniments and sauces for them.

MATJES HERRING

with apples and onions

Serves 4

1³/₄ lb (800 g)	*Matjes fillets*
2	*gherkins, finely chopped*
2	*apples, cored and finely chopped*
1	*onion, cut in rings*
1	*bay leaf*
1¹/₄ cups (300 ml)	*light cream*
1¹/₄ cups (300 ml)	*sour cream*
	Salt
	Sugar
	Pepper
¹/₂ tbsp	*lemon juice*

Step by step

Wash the Matjes fillets under running water and pat dry with paper towels.

For the sauce, mix the light cream and sour cream with salt, sugar, pepper, and lemon juice, and stir thoroughly.

With a sharp knife, cut the Matjes fillets into bite-size pieces.

Pour the sauce over the herring and gently mix the ingredients together.

Put the herring in a bowl with the gherkins, apples, onion, and bay leaf.

Cover and marinate in the icebox for a few hours.

MATJES INFO

Only very young herring can be used for **Matjes** because they still have sufficient fat reserves. They must have at least 15 percent fat.

These herring are preserved in a very special way. When they are gutted, the pancreas is not removed; so, within a few days, the reaction of the enzymes from this gland with a little salt makes the fish deliciously tender and helps it to retain its fine, tangy flavor.

GHERKINS INFO

The classic way of pickling **gherkins** is to steep the young, unripe gherkins, a relative of the cucumber, in a mixture of vinegar and herbs. The pickling

liquid often includes dill, white mustard seeds, vinegar, herbs, onions, salt, and possibly sugar, as well as seasonings such as pepper. For mustard gherkins, on the other hand, medium-sized cucumbers are used, which are also pickled in a special vinegar and mustard mixture. Salted or sour gherkins are preserved by fermentation in lactic acid.

MATJES HERRING
several variations

Most people know the classic way of serving Matjes with gherkins, apples, and onions, the recipe for which can be found on the two preceding pages. But there are one or two other ways of preparing them that taste at least as good.

... with eggs, tarragon, and sorrel

Mix together 11 oz (300 g) each crème fraîche and quark with 1 teaspoon honey and 1 tablespoon mustard. Mix in 2 hard-boiled eggs, chopped very small, 1 finely chopped shallot, 3 tablespoons chopped tarragon, 2 tablespoons chopped chives, and 1 tablespoon chopped sorrel. Fold in the pieces of Matjes fillet and leave to draw in the icebox for a few hours.

... with vinegar, mustard seeds, and pimento

Bring generous $^3/_4$ cup (200 ml) white wine vinegar, $^2/_3$ cup (150 ml) water, 6 tablespoons sugar, 2 teaspoons mustard seeds, 2 teaspoons pimento, 2 bay leaves, and 1 onion cut into rings to a boil and simmer over low heat for a further 5–10 minutes. Allow the liquid to cool a little and pour over the fish. Leave to draw in the icebox for at least 2 days.

... with curry, scallions, and russet apples

Mix together 1 bunch scallions in thin rounds and $1^1/_2$ finely chopped russet apples with 1 cup (250 g) each crème fraîche and yogurt, and 7 tablespoons (100 ml) milk. Season with 2 teaspoons curry powder, salt, pepper, and 3 teaspoons mustard. Fold in the pieces of Matjes fillet, cover, and leave to draw for a few hours in the icebox.

... with red wine vinegar and red onions

Bring 2 cups (500 ml) red wine vinegar to a boil with 1 cup (250 ml) water, 1 cup and 2 tablespoons (250 g) sugar, 2 bay leaves, 1 tablespoon pepper, and $^1/_4$ teaspoon fennel seeds. Cut 2 red onions in rings and add to the pan. Allow to cool. Fold in the pieces of Matjes fillet and leave to draw for a few hours in the icebox.

... with juniper and pearl onions

Cut 8 pearl onions into rings and sweat in a little oil until transparent. Add 1$\frac{1}{2}$ teaspoons crushed juniper berries and 2 bay leaves and sauté briefly, then stir in 1 cup (250 g) crème fraîche and season with salt and lemon juice. Boil for 3 minutes without the lid, then leave to cool. Fold in the pieces of Matjes fillet and leave to draw for a few hours in the icebox.

... with mustard gherkins, radishes, and arugula

Mix together 12 oz (350 g) quark, 1 cup (250 ml) sour cream, and 6 tablespoons liquid from the gherkins. Season with plenty of salt and pepper. Fold in 1 cup and 2 tablespoons (200 g) finely chopped mustard gherkins, 1 bunch sliced radishes, 1 bunch chopped arugula, and 2 red onions sliced into rings. Fold the pieces of Matjes fillet into the mixture and leave to draw in the icebox for about 45 minutes.

SIDE DISHES
for Matjes

As suits the Dutch origins of Matjes, it is served with potatoes, the favorite vegetable in that part of the world, variously prepared—either classically boiled or cooked in a variety of other ways.

Pommes boulangère

Grease a pan with butter and garlic. Line with thin slices of raw potato, cover with sautéed onion rings, pepper, and salt, then with a second layer of potato. Pour over bouillon, and cook in the oven for 50–60 minutes at 350 °F/180 °C.

Boiled potatoes

Scrub waxy potatoes thoroughly under running water. Boil for about 20 minutes in plenty of salt water, drain thoroughly, peel, and serve.

Salted potatoes

Peel the potatoes then wash and cut them into halves or quarters. Cover with just enough salt water and boil for about 20 minutes until soft. After cooking, turn off the heat and leave the pan uncovered to allow the steam to escape.

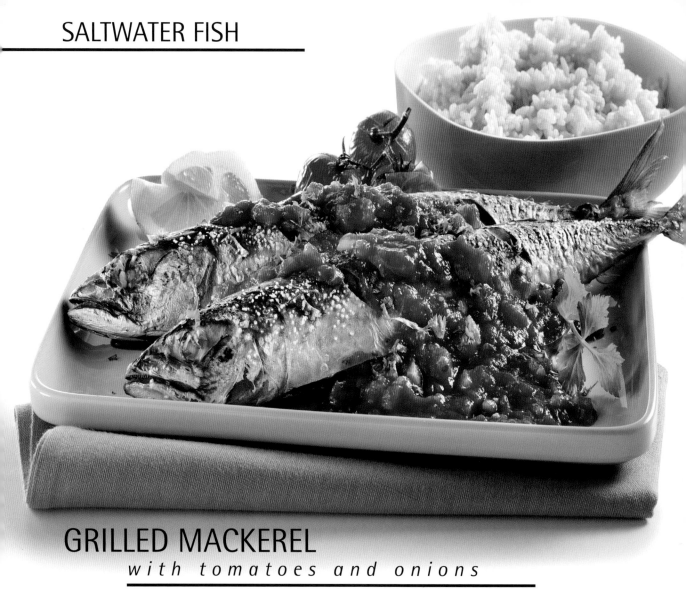

GRILLED MACKEREL
with tomatoes and onions

INFO

The aromatic leaves of the **bay tree** are used to flavor pickled cucumbers and herring, aspic, rubs for meat, and for flavored vinegars—and, of course, for seasoning many meat, fish, and vegetable dishes. Bay leaves are never eaten; they are removed from the dish before serving. Tip: the dried leaves develop their flavor even better if they are torn a little before use.

Serves 4

4	*mackerel, ready to cook*
	Salt
6 tbsp	*oil*
1 large	*onion, finely chopped*
4	*garlic cloves, crushed*
5	*tomatoes, diced*
1 tsp	*Tabasco® Sauce*
1	*bay leaf*
1 bunch	*parsley, chopped*
	Pepper
7 tbsp (100 ml)	*sieved tomatoes*

Step by step

Wash the mackerel, pat dry, and make 3–4 diagonal cuts in each side. Salt and brush with 2 tablespoons of olive oil.

Grill the mackerel on a hot barbecue for 8 minutes on each side.

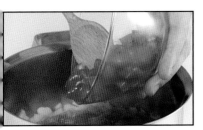

Heat the remaining oil and fry the onion and garlic. Add the diced tomatoes, Tabasco® Sauce, and bay leaf.

After 10 minutes, add the chopped parsley, simmer for 10 minutes, and season with salt and pepper.

Transfer the grilled mackerel to an oven-proof dish and pour over the tomato sauce. Bake for about 15 minutes at 400 °F/200 °C.

Side dish

A spicy **rice** goes well with this dish. Sweat 1 finely chopped onion in a little oil until transparent, add 1¹/₄ cups (250 g) rice to the pan, and fry until lightly browned. Then pour over 2 cups (500 ml) bouillon spiced with chile oil. Stir, transfer to an ovenproof dish, cover, and cook in a preheated oven for 25–30 minutes at 340 °F/175 °C.

Side dish

For another tasty accompaniment to mackerel, you can try **ribbon pasta.** Boil 14 oz (400 g) green ribbon pasta al dente in salted water. While they are cooking, lightly brown 1 chopped onion and 1 chopped garlic clove in 4 tablespoons oil. Peel 7 oz (200 g) tomatoes then deseed, dice, and brown them lightly. Pour over 7 tablespoons (100 ml) white wine and reduce. Season with salt and pepper. Stir in 2¹/₂ oz (75 g) pitted and halved black olives. Drain the noodles and fold into the tomato and olive mixture.

SALADS
for mackerel

A salad or fruit and vegetable tartare always go well with grilled fish. Here are some ideas for your next barbecue:

Red cabbage and apple salad
Shred red cabbage and mix with grated, tart apple and lemon juice. Stir into a dressing made of wine vinegar, salt, white pepper, and light cream.

Wild herb salad
Cut dandelion and sorrel in strips and hand shred some watercress. Stir into a mixture of oil, vinegar, a little salt, pepper, sugar, and finely chopped chervil.

Mango and cucumber tartare
Mix together finely diced mango and cucumber. Add thinly sliced scallion rings. Mix in finely chopped cilantro, salt, and pepper, and leave to draw for 30 minutes without covering.

GRILLED MACKEREL
severa

Mackerel are suitable for almost all preparation methods. Grilled, fried, or boiled, they are always a delicacy. Because of their high fat content of about 12 percent, they are also suitable for smoking, as the heat does not cause the flesh to dry out. Here

... in coconut milk, turmeric, and lemon juice
Brown 1 red onion cut into rings in hot oil. Add 2 crushed garlic cloves, 1 teaspoon turmeric, the juice of $^1/_2$ lemon, and 1 cup (250 ml) coconut milk, cover, and cook for 10 minutes. Then add 1 stick chopped cabanossi (e.g. pepperoni) and the grilled mackerel and cook for about 3 minutes. Turn the mackerel and cook for a further 3 minutes.

... in dashi, mirin, and soy sauce
Bring 7 tablespoons (100 ml) dashi, $3^1/_2$ tablespoons (50 ml) mirin, and $3^1/_2$ tablespoons (50 ml) Japanese soy sauce to a boil. Add $3^1/_2$ oz (100 g) onion rings and the grilled mackerel. Leave to warm through for 10–15 minutes without a lid. Serve the mackerel with the sauce, grated Japanese pickled radish, and ginger.

ariations

are a few suggestions for grilled mackerel, which are either first steeped in a spicy marinade and then barbecued or simply grilled and added to a dish, to which you want to give that inimitable barbecue flavor.

... with parsley, dill, and garlic

For the marinade, grind 3 teaspoons peppercorns in a mortar with salt, pepper, 1 bunch finely chopped parsley, $1/2$ bunch finely chopped dill, and 3 crushed garlic cloves. Mix with the juice of 1 lemon and 6 tablespoons oil. Rub the fish inside and out with the mixture and marinate for at least 30 minutes. Grill the fish, basting occasionally with the marinade.

... with bacon and herbs

Stuff the mackerel with 1 bunch finely chopped mixed herbs. Mix 2 crushed garlic cloves with 8 tablespoons olive oil and the juice of 1 lemon and rub the mackerel with the mixture. Wrap 4 slices bacon round the mackerel, rub the fish with the marinade again, and grill.

SALADS
for mackerel

Substantial, spicy, or fresh—these salads are a perfect complement to grilled or fried fish.

Potato and cucumber salad

Fry onion rings in oil with chopped garlic. Pour over a little bouillon and wine vinegar and season with salt, pepper, and sugar. Mix boiled potatoes and sliced cucumber with the sauce and leave to draw for a short time.

Bell pepper salad

Cut red and green bell peppers in very fine strips and cut an onion into rings. Mix a marinade from lemon juice, salt, pepper, sugar, and oil and fold in the bell peppers and onion.

Feta salad

Mix strips of green bell pepper, onion rings, cubes of Feta, and strips of cucumber with coarsely ground pepper, vinegar, and oil.

FILLETS OF FISH
fried in a beer batter

Serves 4

4	*fish fillets (e.g. cod, ocean perch; about 6¹/₂ oz/180 g each)*
	Lemon juice
	Salt
	Pepper
scant 1¹/₄ cups (180 g)	*all-purpose flour*
2	*eggs, separated*
1 tbsp	*oil*
generous ³/₄ cup (200 ml)	*beer*
2 cups (500 ml)	*oil for frying*

INFO

The art of **deep frying**—cooking submerged in fat—also needs to be learnt. The temperature of the oil plays an important part, so it is sensible to use a deep fryer where you can set the temperature. The temperature should be between 340 °F and 350 °F/170 °C and 180 °C. At lower temperatures, the food absorbs too much fat, while it can quickly burn if the temperature is too high.

Step by step

Pat the fish fillets dry and cut into pieces. Season with lemon juice, salt, and pepper.

Mix together the flour, egg yolks, 1 table-spoon of oil, and the beer, and season with salt and pepper. Beat the egg whites stiffly and fold into the batter.

Roll the fish fillets in flour on both sides and shake off the surplus.

Heat the oil in a heavy skillet or deep fryer to 340–350 °F/170–180 °C.

Dip the fillets one at a time in the batter and fry for about 5 minutes in the deep fat.

Drain the fish on paper towels and serve immediately.

Salad

A refreshing **potato and cucumber salad** is absolutely wonderful with fried fish. Boil 1³/₄ lb (800 g) potatoes and allow to cool. Cut 2 large onions into rings and fry lightly in oil with 1 crushed garlic clove.

Pour over a little bouillon and 5 table-spoons wine vinegar, and season with salt, pepper, and sugar. Slice the potatoes and 1 peeled cucumber and mix with the sauce in a bowl. Allow to draw for a short time.

INFO

Cucumbers are excellent for slimming as they contain very few calories and also many minerals that have a dehydrating effect, reduce fat, and regulate blood sugar. This makes them an ideal accompaniment to salve the conscience when enjoying deep-fried foods. Because of their high water content and minerals, they even make good moisturizing face masks. Cucumber is simply healthy in every way. Cucumbers are available all year round, either outdoor-grown or from glasshouses, depending on the season.

DIPS

for fish fillets

With fried fish fillets it is best to serve dips, mayonnaises, or sauces with a firmer consistency, so the coating remains crisp.

Rémoulade dip

Mix together egg yolk, salt, pepper, sugar, vinegar, and mustard. Gradually stir in oil. Mix in finely chopped gherkins, capers, chopped anchovies, and finely chopped parsley. Goes well with the fish in beer batter, pecorino and rosemary, and herb coating recipes.

Mustard dip

Stir together yogurt, medium-hot mustard, and Italian herbs until smooth. Season with salt and pepper. Goes well with the fish in beer batter, pecorino and rosemary, and herb coating variations.

Olive dip

Purée cream cheese and pickled bell peppers. Stir in Parmesan, salad cream, or mayonnaise, finely chopped, pitted black olives, and crushed garlic. Season with salt and pepper. Goes well with the fish in beer batter, pecorino and rosemary, and herb coating recipes.

FISH FILLETS

severa

Various kinds of fish are suitable for these recipes. The most common, which can be found in the deep-freeze aisles of every good supermarket, are cod and the various types of rockfish, including ocean perch, also known as rose- or redfish. These are reasonably-priced fish, so they are suitable for everyday meals.

... with a peanut butter and chile coating

Season the fish fillets with salt and pepper. Beat 1 egg until frothy and mix with 2 tablespoons peanut butter. Add 3 table-spoons flour and 5 tablespoons milk, pepper, salt, chile powder, and 1 tablespoon chopped cilantro, and stir to form a thick batter. Dip the pieces of fish in the batter and deep fry in hot oil until golden brown.

... with a pecorino and rosemary coating

Season the fish fillets with salt and pepper, toss in 4 tables-poons flour, and shake off the loose flour. Mix 1 tablespoon chopped rosemary leaves with 1 beaten egg and plenty of freshly ground black pepper. Dip the fish in the rosemary and egg mixture first, then in scant 1 cup (100 g) finely grated pecorino. Deep fry in hot fat until golden brown.

...ariations

All the variations here can be made with these species of fish. Incidentally, when using frozen foods, remember to include the thawing time when planning. Cut the fish fillets into small, bite-size pieces, which will reduce the frying time to a few minutes for all variations.

... with a coconut coating

Rub the fillets with the juice of 1 lemon, salt, and pepper. Roll in a little flour, then in beaten egg, and finally in a mixture of 4 tablespoons grated coconut and 2 tablespoons bread-crumbs. Deep fry in hot fat until golden brown.

... with a herb coating

Mix together 5¹/₂ oz (150 g) finely crumbed wholemeal bread, without crusts, with 1 bunch each finely chopped chives and parsley. Beat 1 egg with 4 tablespoons water. Drizzle the fish fillets with lemon juice and season with salt and pepper. Dip first in 4 tablespoons flour, then in the egg, and finally in the breadcrumbs. Press lightly and deep fry in clarified butter.

SIDE DISHES
for fish fillets

Fried potatoes taste good with crisply fried fish fillets.

Pommes dauphinoise

Bring water to a boil with a little butter, salt, and nutmeg, and remove from the heat. Stir in a little flour, return the pan to the heat, and form into a dumpling. Stir in eggs and mashed potato. Make small balls of the mixture and deep fry until golden brown

Carrot and potato rösti

Mix coarsely grated, leftover boiled potatoes with half the quantity of grated carrot, and season with salt. Brown in butter and press together in cakes. Cover and fry over low heat until golden brown. Flip over and fry on the other side until golden brown.

Grisons-style potatoes

Coarsely grate leftover boiled potatoes. Mix with flour and season with salt. Fry in lard for 30 minutes, stirring constantly. Gradually add more lard. Sprinkle with flakes of butter before serving.

CRÈME FRAÎCHE INFO

Crème fraîche is an extremely rich, firm, sour cream, which has the great advantage of not curdling when heated so it can

be used in cooking without any problems. It gives dishes a pleasant, slightly sour note, while at the same time producing a creamy consistency. With its minimum fat content of 30 percent, however, it also contains a high number of calories and is not an ingredient to use in everyday cooking.

ALUMINUM FOIL INFO

Cooking in **aluminum foil** is not only a good way of cooking delicate fish, it is also suitable for meat, vegetables, and fruit that need to be carefully cooked in their own juices with no, or only a little, additional fat and/or liquid. The food becomes crisp

and brown without drying out, most of the vitamins and nutrients are retained—and, what is more, cooking odors are not released into the kitchen and the oven does not get dirty. Always take care that the matt side of the foil is on the outside, as the shiny, heat-repellent side slows down the cooking process.

Serves 4

2 tbsp	*lemon juice*
1 tbsp	*Cognac*
3 tbsp	*mixed fresh herbs, chopped*
	Salt
	Pepper
3 tbsp	*oil*
4	*fish fillets (e.g. cod or redfish, each about 6$^1/_2$ oz/180 g)*
	Aluminum foil
	Butter for the foil
2	*tomatoes, peeled and sliced*
4 tbsp	*crème fraîche*

Step by step

Make a marinade by mixing together the lemon juice, Cognac, herbs, salt, pepper, and oil.

Cover the fish with slices of tomato, drizzle with a little marinade, and brush with crème fraîche.

Rub the fish fillets with the marinade then marinate for 20 minutes in the icebox.

Wrap in foil, so no juice can escape. Fold the edges over several times.

Brush the shiny side of 4 pieces of aluminum foil with a little butter and lay the pieces of fish on top.

Bake for 15–20 minutes at 400 °F/200 °C. The fish is ready when the foil parcels begin to swell.

FISH FILLETS IN FOIL
with tomatoes and herbs

SAUCES
for fish in foil

Here you can put your heart into it, as spicy sauces are sometimes the perfect complement for fish with a delicate flavor.

Bell pepper and pecan sauce

Place the bell pepper, skin side up, on a baking sheet and bake for about 20 minutes. Remove the skin and roughly chop the flesh. Purée with garlic, chile, pecans, white bread, cumin, sugar, salt, pepper, and lemon juice, while gradually adding oil.

Sauce tartare

Mix together mayonnaise, capers, finely chopped hard-boiled egg, finely chopped gherkins, onion, and chopped parsley. Goes well with all variations.

Walnut sauce

Dry fry finely diced pita bread. Pulse in a blender with roughly chopped walnuts. Stir in finely chopped parsley, plenty of olive oil, some water, and salt. Goes well with all variations.

... with leek, carrots, and mushrooms

Thinly slice 2 carrots, 1 leek, and $1^3/_4$ oz (50 g) mushrooms and dice 2 large tomatoes. Arrange the vegetables on aluminum foil and season with salt and pepper. Drizzle the fish fillets with lemon juice, season with salt and pepper, and place them on the vegetables. Top with a few flakes of butter and 2 crushed garlic cloves, close up the foil, and bake in the oven for 15–20 minutes.

... with potatoes, bell pepper, and beefsteak tomatoes

Arrange 8 sliced, boiled potatoes on the foil. Drizzle the fish with lemon, season with salt and pepper, and lay them on the potato. Cover the fillets with 2 sliced beefsteak tomatoes, 2 red bell peppers cut into strips, and 4 onions cut into segments. Season with salt, pepper, chile powder, and garlic. Close up the foil and bake in the oven for 15–20 minutes.

FISH FILLETS IN FOIL
several variations

Cooking fish in foil is a gentle method that is particularly good for retaining both nutrients and flavor. It is suitable for fish fillets and also for small, whole fish.

... with zucchini, cherry tomatoes, and Feta

Drizzle the fillets with lemon juice and season with salt and pepper. Mix together 1 sliced zucchini, 7 oz (200 g) halved cherry tomatoes, 2 onions cut into rings, 2 crushed garlic cloves, 7 oz (200 g) Feta cubes, and 1³/₄ oz (50 g) bacon, and season with salt and pepper. Spread on aluminum foil, season with chile powder, arrange the fish on top, close up the foil, and bake in the oven for 15–20 minutes.

... with dill, parsley, and herb butter

Drizzle the fish fillets with lemon juice and season with salt and pepper. Arrange the fillets on aluminum foil, and spread with a mixture of 1 teaspoon ground mustard seeds, ¹/₂ bunch each chopped dill and chopped parsley, and 1 teaspoon herb butter. Top each with 1 slice lemon. Close up the foil and cook in the oven for 15–20 minutes.

... with gherkins, bacon, and onion

Cut fish fillets into three and season with vinegar, salt, and pepper. Place 1 piece of fillet on aluminum foil and top with 1 diced gherkin and a second piece of fish. Fry 1³/₄ oz (50 g) diced bacon, add 1 chopped onion and 2 bunches chopped dill, and spread over the fish. Place a third piece of fish on top, and cover with 1 oz (25 g) diced bacon. Close up the foil, and cook in the oven for 15–20 minutes.

... with Swiss chard, bolete, and shrimp

Sweat the leaves and chopped stems of 14 oz (400 g) Swiss chard. Arrange on aluminum foil. Cover with 9 oz (250 g) each sliced common-store mushrooms and soaked bolete, 3¹/₂ oz (100 g) halved shrimp, and 1 chile cut into quarters. Arrange the fish fillets on top and cover with rosemary and thyme. Drizzle with generous ³/₄ cup (200 ml) white wine and 4 tablespoons olive oil. Close up the foil, and bake in the oven for 15–20 minutes.

FISH RAGOUT
with bolete and zucchini

Serves 4

7 oz (200 g)	*cod fillet*
7 oz (200 g)	*ocean perch fillet*
7 oz (200 g)	*bocaccio fillet*
2 tbsp	*lemon juice*
	Salt
	Pepper
1	*onion, finely chopped*
9 oz (250 g)	*bolete, soaked and thinly sliced*
2 tbsp	*butter*
2	*zucchini, roughly chopped*
³/₄ cup (200 ml)	*white wine*
1 cup (250 ml)	*fish bouillon (bottled)*
10 tbsp (150 g)	*crème fraîche*
1 bunch	*dill, finely chopped*

Step by step

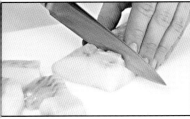

Wash the fish fillets, pat dry, and cut into large cubes. Drizzle with lemon juice, season with salt and pepper, and refrigerate.

Stir in the crème fraîche, season with salt and pepper, and simmer for about 10 minutes.

Sweat the onion and bolete in butter for 5 minutes, then add the chopped zucchini.

Add the fish and simmer in the sauce for about 5 minutes, until tender.

Pour over the white wine and reduce a little. Add the fish bouillon.

Add chopped dill and season the sauce again with salt and pepper, if required.

RAGOUT INFO

The word **"ragout"** describes a dish consisting of pieces of boiled or steamed meat, fish, or mushrooms and other

ingredients in a—usually smooth and piquant—sauce. Unlike meat, which must first be cooked separately from the other ingredients because of its longer cooking time, pieces of fish, which cook quite quickly, are simply added to the sauce toward the end, and only need to simmer gently in it for a few minutes. It is important in this case to ensure the sauce does not boil, as otherwise the delicate pieces of fish will quickly disintegrate.

DILL INFO

Dill is a favorite herb to go with fish dishes, but it is also popular in salads, in sauces based on oil, yogurt, or quark, and in herb butter. It is also an important ingredient for pickling gherkins. Dill is available both fresh and dried, but has a much stronger

flavor when used fresh. Sprigs of dill are mainly used fresh, dried, frozen, or freeze-dried.

FISH RAGOUT
several variations

The taste of the actual fish is of lesser importance here, because the many different flavors of individual ingredients in a ragout all contribute. So in these recipes you can use fillets of the cheaper saltwater fish varieties.

... with shrimp and bacon

Sauté 2 finely chopped shallots with 3^1/$_2$ oz (100 g) diced bacon in 4 tablespoons clarified butter. Dust with 1 teaspoon flour and stir in generous ^{3}/$_4$ cup (200 ml) white wine. Dissolve the contents of 1 sachet saffron in 1 cup (250 ml) light cream, add to the pan, and simmer briefly. Add the fish, and simmer gently for a few minutes. Shortly before serving, add 7 oz (200 g) cooked shrimp.

... with cured ham and shiitake mushrooms

Lightly brown 3^1/$_2$ oz (100 g) diced cured ham. Sauté 1 crushed garlic clove, 1 bunch chopped scallions, 14 oz (400 g) diced celery, and 14 oz (400 g) sliced shiitake mushrooms in the same skillet. Add 7 oz (200 g) silverskin onions, 1 bay leaf, and lemon rind. Add generous ^{3}/$_4$ cup (200 ml) red wine and reduce. Add 2^1/$_2$ cups (600 ml) fish bouillon and heat. Add the fish and simmer gently for a few minutes.

... with gherkins and capers

Lightly brown 3 tablespoons flour in 3 tablespoons butter. Pour over 1^2/$_3$ cups (400 ml) milk, add the fish, and simmer gently for 10–15 minutes. Add 14 oz (400 g) diced gherkins and 4 tablespoons capers. Enrich with 7 tablespoons (100 ml) light cream. Season with salt, pepper, dill, and 1 pinch sugar.

... with curry, coconut milk, and peas

Season pieces of fish with salt and pepper, drizzle with lemon juice, and brown lightly. Sprinkle with 2 teaspoons curry powder. Pour over 7 tablespoons (100 ml) each vegetable bouillon and light cream, and ^{2}/$_3$ cup (150 ml) coconut milk. Add canned mandarins and canned peas, 1 tablespoon oyster sauce, 3^1/$_2$ oz (100 g) precooked shrimp, and 2 tablespoons chopped parsley. Add mandarin juice, salt and pepper to taste, and sprinkle with toasted, grated coconut.

SIDE DISHES
for fish ragout

Rice goes with all versions of ragout. Incidentally, the nutty taste of wild rice mixtures is delicious as well.

... with carrots and potatoes

Sauté generous 1 lb (500 g) peeled and quartered potatoes. Cut 1³/₄ (750 g) carrots into strips, add to the potatoes, and season with salt and pepper. Pour over 1¹/₂ cups (375 ml) fish bouillon and 1 cup (250 ml) light cream, and cook for 15 minutes. Add 1 bunch chopped scallions, cook for a further 5 minutes, season with salt and pepper, and thicken. Add the fish and simmer gently for a few minutes. Mix in 1 bunch finely chopped dill.

.. with leek and lemon

Salt the fish fillets and marinate in the juice of 2 lemons. Sweat chopped onions in a little butter, but do not brown. Add the fish and the marinade and 2¹/₄ lb (1 kg) washed leeks, still wet and cut into thin rounds. Cook gently for about 30 minutes, and season with salt and pepper.

Butter rice

Sweat 1¹/₄ cups (250 g) rice in butter with chopped onion until transparent. Pour over 2¹/₂ cups (600 ml) bouillon and add salt. Allow the rice to swell for 20 minutes over low heat, then stir in flakes of butter.

Risi-bisi

Sweat 1¹/₄ cups (250 g) rice in butter with chopped onion until transparent. Pour over 2¹/₂ cups (600 ml) bouillon and add frozen peas. Season with salt. Allow the rice to swell for 20 minutes over low heat. Break up the rice with a fork and allow the steam to disperse.

Zucchini rice

Sweat 1¹/₄ cups (250 g) rice in butter with chopped onion until transparent. Pour over 2¹/₂ cups (600 ml) bouillon and add salt. Allow the rice to swell for 20 minutes over low heat. Mix in lightly cooked, shredded zucchini, and grated Gouda.

79

HERBES DE PROVENCE INFO

Herbes de Provence can be bought ready-mixed in most food stores. The mixture consists mainly of thyme, rosemary, bay, lavender, winter savory, oregano, and sage, and originated in Provence in the southwest of

France, where these plants grow wild. Other mixtures contain fennel seeds, but not bay or savory. You can buy the mixture fresh, dried, or preserved in pickling vinegar or oil.

OLIVES INFO

Because of their bitter taste, **olives** are inedible when raw, but after being steeped several times in a solution of caustic soda to flush out the bitter substances and then pickled in lactic acid, they are good to eat. Olives are sold dry, in water, vinegar, or

brine, with or without herbs and spices. The larger ones may also be stuffed. Unripe—that is, green—olives are harvested in October; the ripe fruits are brown, red, or purplish-black and are gathered from December through January. Some green olives are dyed black, however, with ferrous gluconate.

Serves 4

1³/₄ lb (800 g)	*monkfish medallions*
	Olive oil
2 tbsp	*butter*
	Salt
	Pepper
2	*garlic cloves*
20	*pitted black olives*
1 tbsp	*herbes de Provence*
4 bunches	*cherry tomatoes on the vine*

Step by step

Wash the monkfish medallions and pat dry with paper towels. Brown lightly in oil. When they begin to brown, add butter.

Brush the cherry tomatoes on the vine with olive oil. Place on a baking sheet and cook in the oven for 10 minutes at 400 °F/200 °C, until the skins split.

Turn the fish and fry for 3 minutes. Remove from the pan, season with salt and pepper, and keep warm.

Remove the tomatoes from the baking sheet and sprinkle with salt and pepper.

Crush the garlic cloves in their skins. Sweat in the fish pan together with the olives and herbes de Provence.

Arrange the monkfish medallions on plate with the olives and the tomatoes, still on the vine, beside them.

FRIED MONKFISH
with cherry tomatoes and olives

SIDE DISHES
for monkfish

Spicy or mild vegetable accompaniments are suitable, depending on how the fish is prepared. Here are three, summery suggestions:

Runner beans
Cut runner beans into pieces diagonally and cook in boiling, salt water until tender. Drain, mix with melted butter, and season with salt and pepper.

Savoy cabbage
Cut the cabbage leaves into strips and blanch for 2 minutes in salt water. Sauté chopped shallots in butter until transparent and mix with salt, pepper, nutmeg, and lemon juice. Add the béchamel sauce to the cabbage and warm through.

Vegetable medley
Chop broccoli, asparagus, sugar snap peas, and scallions into pieces and cook until al dente. Lightly brown scallions and cherry tomatoes in butter. Add a little balsamic vinegar and the other vegetables, combine thoroughly, and season with salt and pepper.

FRIED MONKFISH
severa

Monkfish has beautiful, firm flesh, which is perfect for frying in medallions. It can either be lightly browned, or not browned but simply cooked gently in a sauce until tender. Alternatively, it can be pan-fried. You can find both methods in these

... with mango, lime, and chile
Lightly brown 1 finely chopped chile and drizzle with the juice of 1 lime. Reduce $1^2/_3$ cups (400 ml) fish bouillon and 7 tablespoons (100 ml) white wine by two-thirds, and add 7 tablespoons (100 ml) light cream. Simmer with grated lime peel. Cut 2 mangoes into quarters and fry in butter. Keep warm. Add the fish medallions to the pan, pour over the sauce, and warm through for a few minutes.

... with Parma ham and sage
Score the medallions lengthways, without cutting right through Fill each medallion with 1 slice Parma ham and 2 sage leaves and secure with cocktail picks. Cover and refrigerate. Season with salt and pepper and fry for 3 minutes on each side. Remove from the pan and keep warm. Heat 3 tablespoons butter in the pan until frothy, add 8 sage leaves, and serve with the fish.

ariations

variations—fruity and exotic or fruity Provençal-style, and even spicy with ham or sauerkraut. With this fish, you can use any mild- or strong-flavored accompaniment, according to taste. Choose from the suggestions on the left and serve with rice or bulgur.

... with orange, honey, and lavender

Season the monkfish with salt and pepper and fry fiercely in olive oil on both sides for in 3–5 minutes, until tender. Keep warm. Add 2 chopped oranges, 4 tablespoons honey, and 2 teaspoons green peppercorns to the pan juices and toss thoroughly. Add a few lavender flowers. Serve the fish with the sauce.

... with sauerkraut, Riesling, and smoked bacon

Warm 14 oz (400 g) sauerkraut in a pan and pour over 7 tablespoons (100 ml) Riesling. Add 2 finely chopped shallots to the same quantity of Riesling and reduce by half. Add 7 tablespoons (100 ml) beef bouillon and generous ³/₄ cup (200 ml) light cream, and reduce to a creamy sauce. Spike the medallions with 3 oz (80 g) finely diced smoked bacon and fry in oil and butter on the spiked side. Turn and simmer for a few minutes, until tender. Serve with sauerkraut and sauce.

SIDE DISHES
for monkfish

These three ways of preparing rice are the perfect complement for the monkfish variations.

Colorful risotto

Cook 1¹/₂ cups (300 g) risotto rice and mix in pitted and chopped black olives, sun-dried tomatoes, and chopped scallions. Goes well with monkfish with Parma ham, and sauerkraut.

Mixed rice with chile and leek

Cook 1¹/₄ cups (250 g) rice/wild rice mixture in double the quantity of salt water. Cut 1 red chile into rounds and 1 leek into strips, sweat in oil, and mix with the rice. Goes well with monkfish with mango, and sauerkraut.

Bulgur with bell pepper, tomatoes, and basil

Prepare 1¹/₄ cups (250 g) bulgur. Mix with diced red and green bell peppers, diced tomatoes, and strips of basil. Goes wekk with monkfish with mango, and orange.

83

ROCKFISH
with mushrooms wrapped in Savoy cabba

INFO

Curry powder is not the same thing as curry. In the country where it originated, the Tamil word does not mean the spices, but the method of preparing meat, fish, and vegetables in sauce. In Germany and other places, the word "curry" is used for a mixture of spices, which is actually not used in Indian cuisine. Indians call their spice mixtures "masalas." The yellow turmeric root is an important component, which gives the powder its typical yellow color and characteristic taste.

Serves 4

16	pale green Savoy cabbage leaves
	Salt
4 tsp	flour
3 tsp	ground wasabi
4	rockfish fillets (each about 6 oz/170 g)
6 tsp	oil
5 1/2 oz (150 g)	mushrooms, diced
	Pepper

Step by step

Blanch the cabbage in salt water and rinse in running water. Cut out the stalks, and press the leaves flat between paper towels.

Mix together the flour and wasabi. Salt the fish and toss in the flour. Shake off the loose flour.

Brown the fish in hot oil over medium heat for about $1/2$–1 minute on each side.

Lay each piece of fish on 2 cabbage leaves, spread the mushrooms on top, and sprinkle with salt and pepper.

Cover with the remaining cabbage leaves and tie with kitchen string. Cook in the oven for 20 minutes at 400 °F/200 °C.

Side dishes

Curry and turmeric rice also has the flavor of Asia about it. First, sweat $1^1/_4$ cups (250 g) long-grain rice in 4 tablespoons butter, until transparent. Add 1 tablespoon each curry powder and turmeric, pour over double the quantity of liquid (preferably chicken bouillon), add salt, and leave the rice to swell over low heat for 20 minutes. Then let the steam escape and stir in 2 table-spoons flaked butter.

Salad

A **Thai salad** goes well with Asian fish. Cut 1 romaine lettuce and $1/_2$ red bell pepper into strips, and slice $1/_2$ cucumber, 4 small tomatoes, and 2 hard-boiled eggs. For the dressing, grind 2 tablespoons unsalted peanuts to a fine paste and mix with the finely chopped white of 2 lemongrass stems, 4 tablespoons peanut oil, 5 tablespoons lemon juice, 2 teaspoons sambal ulek, and 1 tablespoon honey. Mix everything together and season with coriander, salt, and pepper.

SALTWATER FISH

SAUCES
for rockfish

Even more delicious with a spicy sauce—here, you can choose between an exotic curry and coconut flavor, the heady aroma of red wine, and an even more sophisticated version with sherry and cream.

Sherry cream sauce

Beat together eggs and cream, and reduce. Season with nutmeg and salt. Goes well with rockfish with a potato, Gouda, and chive crust.

Red wine sauce

Add red wine to the pan juices from the fish and reduce a little. Season with salt and pepper, and remove from the heat. Stir in knobs of ice-cold butter and serve immediately. Goes well with rockfish wrapped in Swiss chard, or bacon, and with an oatflake and rosemary crust.

Spinach, curry, and coconut sauce

Lightly brown chopped onion, crushed garlic, finely chopped chile, and curry paste in sesame oil. Pour over fish sauce. Add chopped spinach and allow to wilt. Add coconut milk and season with salt, pepper, and sugar. Goes well with rockfish wrapped in Swiss chard, and with a white bread and ginger crust.

... with a potato, Gouda, and chive crust

Cook the fish for 15 minutes with 1 onion, 1 bay leaf, and $^1/_2$ cup (125 ml) white wine. Cover with a mixture of $1^3/_4$ lb (750 g) puréed boiled potatoes, chopped chives, $5^1/_2$ oz (150 g) Gouda, lemon juice, salt, pepper, and 2 stiffly beaten egg whites, and drizzle with 5 tablespoons melted butter. Bake at 400 °F/200 °C. Strain the fish stock and reduce. Stir in generous $^3/_4$ cup (200 g) crème fraîche.

... in an oatflake and rosemary crust

Crush 4 tablespoons oatflakes and 1 teaspoon rosemary and mix together. Season the fish fillets with salt and pepper and roll in the oatflakes. Press the coating on well. Fry the fillets on one side in oil, remove from the pan, reheat the fat, and then fry on the other side.

ROCKFISH
several variations

In these variations, rockfish fillets are concealed under a crust or cooked in a spicy wrap. This way, you can produce delicious meals with in-built accompaniments.

... with a potato, tomato, and Edam crust

Sweat 1 chopped onion and bring to a boil with 14 oz (400 g) canned tomatoes. Stir in ¹/₂ cup (125 g) crème fraîche and season with salt and pepper. Spread over the fish and top with 4¹/₂ oz (125 g) diced mozzarella. Cover with a purée of generous 1 lb (500 g) boiled potatoes, ¹/₂ cup (125 ml) milk, and butter. Sprinkle with grated Edam and dried breadcrumbs. Bake for about 30 minutes at 400 °F/200 °C.

... wrapped in bacon, with onions

Lightly brown 2 onions sliced into rings, add 1 crushed garlic clove, pour over 2 tablespoons white wine, season with salt and pepper, and sweat until soft. Cut each fillet into three diagonally, drizzle with the juice of 1 lemon, and season with salt and pepper. Wrap each piece of fish in 2 rashers bacon together with 1 teaspoon of the onion mixture and some chopped parsley leaves, secure, and fry.

... in a white bread and ginger crust

Mix together 7 tablespoons (100 g) butter with 1³/₄ oz (50 g) finely grated ginger, a little lemon juice, and 4 slices finely chopped white bread. Season with salt and pepper. Fry the fish in 3 tablespoons lime oil. Spread with the ginger mixture and broil for about 5 minutes.

... wrapped in Swiss chard with Emmental

Arrange 12 Swiss chard leaves overlapping on aluminum foil. Arrange 3 fish fillets, each 1³/₄ oz (50 g), one on top of the other on the chard, with 1 slice Emmental between each. Fold the leaves together and close up the foil. Cook for about 20 minutes at 350 ° F/180 °C. Leave to rest for 5 minutes. Chop and sauté the chard stems. Stir in 2 tablespoons sour cream, purée, and season with salt, pepper, and nutmeg.

TUNA STEAKS
with bell peppers and tomatoes

Serves 4

2	*red bell peppers*
3	*beefsteak tomatoes, peeled and diced small*
1	*chile, finely chopped*
1 bunch	*cilantro, finely chopped*
¹/₂ tsp	*cumin, ground*
	Salt
	Pepper
4	*tuna steaks (each about 6 oz/180 g)*
3 tbsp	*clarified butter*

Step by step

Wrap the bell peppers in aluminum foil and bake for 45 minutes at 350 °F/180 °C. Turn after 10 minutes.

Season with cumin, salt, and pepper, mix, and chill in the icebox for 1 hour.

Allow to cool a little and remove the blistered skin. Dice the flesh.

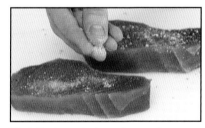

Wash the tuna steaks under running water, pat dry with paper towels, and season with salt and pepper.

Mix the diced bell peppers and tomatoes with the chile and cilantro.

Fry the tuna steaks in clarified butter for 5 minutes on each side. Serve with the vegetables.

SALADS
for tuna

A delicious salad not only gives you lots of vitamins, it gives you a kick as well!

Raw beet salad

Peel raw beet and grate finely. Mix a dressing from vinegar, oil, salt, pepper, sugar, grated horseradish, and ground cumin, and mix with beet. Goes well with tuna with bell peppers and olives, and with rhubarb and port.

Tomato and bell pepper salad

Arrange sliced tomatoes, strips of bell pepper, and onion rings in layers in a bowl. Mix a marinade from oil, lemon juice, salt, and sugar and pour over the vegetable strips. Goes well with the tuna with bell peppers and olives, rhubarb and port, and potatoes and carrots recipe variations.

Spinach salad

Blanch young spinach leaves, rinse in cold water, and leave to drain. Add chopped onions. Mix with a marinade of oil, lemon juice, salt, pepper, and sugar. Goes with all variations.

TUNA STEAKS
severa

Tuna steaks are also perfect for barbecuing. To prevent them from getting dry and help them to absorb delicious flavorings, you should marinate them before grilling in olive oil, to which you can add spices and other flavorings such as lemon juice. Brush the grill rack with oil and put it on the lowest

... with green bell peppers, olives, and tomatoes

Fry the tuna steaks and drizzle with lemon juice. Cover and keep warm. Sweat the rings of 1 onion in oil until transparent. Add 2 crushed garlic cloves, $5^1/_2$ oz (150 g) green bell pepper strips, 7 oz (200 g) stuffed olives, 2 teaspoons each tomato paste and heavy cream, and fry gently. Season with rosemary, thyme, paprika, salt, and pepper.

... with potatoes, carrots, and tandoori spice

Marinate the tuna in $^2/_3$ cup (150 ml) yogurt, oil, lime juice, tandoori masala, garlic, salt, and pepper. In an ovenproof dish, put 6 diced potatoes and 6 diced carrots, 2 diced bell peppers, 1 onion, cut into rings, and a little oil. Season with salt, pepper, lime juice, lime peel, and tandoori masala. Bake for 1 hour at 400 °F/200 °C. Fry the fish for 5 minutes on each side.

ariations

level of the hot barbecue. Grill the steak immediately on one side, until the lower third of the flesh turns pale, then turn, and grill it for the same length of time on the highest level, brushing occasionally with the marinade.

... with rhubarb, port, and balsamic vinegar

Fry the tuna for 5 minutes on each side, cover, and keep warm. For the sauce, add generous $^3/_4$ cup (200 ml) port and 3 tablespoons balsamic vinegar to the pan, mix with the pan juices, and reduce a little. Add 9 oz (250 g) chopped, cooked rhubarb, 1 tablespoon fish sauce, and 1$^1/_4$ cups (300 ml) bouillon, and reduce by half. Season to taste, adding a little sugar if desired.

... with bananas, coconut cream, and lime juice

Purée 2 bananas with 3 tablespoons lime juice, and add 1 tablespoon fish sauce. Fry 1$^3/_4$ oz (50 g) chopped scallions with $^1/_3$ oz (10 g) chopped ginger. Bring to a boil with the banana purée and 1 tablespoon curry powder. Add $^2/_3$ cup (150 ml) coconut cream, reduce, and season with pepper. Sprinkle an ovenproof dish with cilantro, drizzle the fish with lime juice, and arrange on top. Bake for 30 minutes at 300 °F/150 °C, turning occasionally.

SAUCES
for tuna

With grilled, fried, or baked tuna steaks like those in our variations, these sauces are absolutely irresistible.

Tarragon and mustard sauce

Mix the pan juices with white wine, add finely chopped tarragon and mustard, and bring briefly to a boil. Goes well with tuna steak with bell peppers and tomatoes.

Olive sauce

Sweat finely chopped onion in butter until transparent. Pour over red wine, thicken with tomato sauce and light cream, add black olives, and season with salt, pepper, and sugar. Goes well with tuna steak with bell peppers and tomatoes.

Caper and pepper sauce

Sweat finely chopped onion until transparent. Pour over white wine, thicken with pan juices, add capers and green peppercorns, and season with salt, pepper, cayenne, mustard, sugar, and brandy. Goes well with tuna steak with bell peppers and tomatoes.

STUFFED DOLPHINFISH
with tomatoes and zucchini

INFO

Garlic, the ultimate vampire-repellent, is used in both hot and cold cuisine. If you are frying garlic, on no account let it brown, as it will quickly become bitter. However good dishes containing garlic may taste, many people find the smell of garlic on the breath of those who have eaten it very unpleasant. There are countless household remedies for such odors, but their effectiveness is disputed.

Serves 4

generous 1 lb (500 g)	tomatoes, in quarters
1 bunch	scallions, chopped
11 oz (300 g)	zucchini, diced
3½ oz (100 g)	pitted black olives
4½ oz (125 g)	sun-dried tomatoes, finely chopped
1 bunch	thyme, chopped
1 bunch	basil, chopped
4	garlic cloves
4	dolphinfish, ready to cook
	Salt
	Pepper
¾ cup (200 ml)	white wine
3 tbsp	olive oil
1	lemon

Step by step

Grease an ovenproof dish and line with the tomatoes, scallions, zucchini, and olives.

Mix together 3 tablespoons of sun-dried tomatoes, $^1/_2$ bunch thyme, the basil, and 1 crushed garlic clove.

Wash the dolphinfish, pat dry, and season with salt and pepper. Stuff with the mixture and arrange on the bed of vegetables.

Top with the remaining garlic, thyme, and sun-dried tomatoes.

Pour over the white wine and drizzle with olive oil. Cook in the oven for 25–30 minutes at 425 °F/220 °C. Serve with the lemon cut into segments.

Salad

A delicious **chicory salad** tastes good with stuffed dolphinfish (also known as mahi mahi, or dorado). Clean and wash 2 chicory, cut in half, remove the bitter core, and slice. Clean and trim $3^1/_2$ oz (100 g) green asparagus, and cook for 15 minutes in a little salt water. Drain and chop. Peel 1 red onion and cut into rings. Clean and slice $^1/_2$ bunch radishes. Mix the ingredients with a dressing of 7 tablespoons sour cream, 2 tablespoons lemon juice, salt, and pepper.

Side dishes

Radicchio and apple mix:
Cut 1 small radicchio into quarters, remove the stalk, and slice. Cut 1 green, unpeeled apple into four, remove the core, and cut into segments. Heat 1 tablespoon butter until it foams, add $^1/_2$ teaspoon confectioners' sugar and the apple, and caramelize lightly. Add the radicchio and juice of 1 lime. Season with salt and simmer for 3 minutes. Add a little water if necessary.

STUFFED DOLPHINFISH
several variations

Because of their size and firm flesh with very few bones, dolphinfish are very good for stuffing. They work well with all kinds of flavors, as can be seen from the different variations.

... with olives and mushrooms

Lightly brown $1\frac{1}{2}$ oz (40 g) chopped shallots in butter with 12 oz (350 g) mushrooms. Add 1 teaspoon tarragon, 6 tablespoons (100 g) crème fraîche, and 12 pitted black olives, and toss together briefly. Stuff the fish with the mixture and fasten with a toothpick. Lay the fish on a baking sheet, brush with a little oil, and cook for 20 minutes at 400 °F/200 °C.

... with spinach and croutons

Clean and blanch 14 oz (400 g) spinach, drain, and chop. Mix with 2 chopped, sautéed shallots, generous $\frac{3}{4}$ cup (200 ml) light cream, and $1\frac{3}{4}$ oz (50 g) cubes of toasted white bread, and season with salt, pepper, and nutmeg. Stuff the fish with the mixture, close up, place on a baking sheet, brush with oil, and bake for 20 minutes at 400 °F/200 °C.

... with celery, bell pepper, and herbs

Stuff the fish with 1 sprig each rosemary and thyme. Lay each fish diagonally on a sheet of parchment paper. Pour 1 tablespoon garlic oil on each fish, scatter each with 1 finely chopped celery stalk and $\frac{1}{2}$ each finely chopped red and yellow bell peppers, and season with salt and pepper. Top each fish with a sprig of rosemary and thyme, and wrap in the parchment paper. Bake for 25–30 minutes at 400 °F/200 °C.

... with zucchini, couscous, and currants

Allow 1 cup (200 g) couscous to swell in $1\frac{1}{2}$ cups (350 ml) bouillon. Clean and dice 2 zucchini and brown lightly in butter. Mix with the couscous, $1\frac{3}{4}$ oz (50 g) currants, and $\frac{1}{4}$ cup (30 g) toasted pine nuts, and season with salt and pepper. Stuff the dolphinfish with the mixture, close up, place on a baking sheet, brush with oil, and bake for 20 minutes at 400 °F/200 °C.

SAUCES
for dolphinfish

A mildly spicy sauce is a fine complement to stuffed dolphinfish. The sauces below are very easy to prepare.

Basil and butter sauce
Heat butter in a small skillet and toss pieces of torn basil leaves in it. Goes well with the dolphinfish with olives and mushrooms, and bolete and parsley recipe variations.

Rosemary and shallot sauce
Lightly brown diced shallots in butter with sprigs of rosemary. Add red wine, then reduce almost completely. Add fish bouillon and reduce again. Thicken with small pieces of ice-cold butter. Goes well with all kinds of stuffed dolphinfish.

White wine and currant sauce
Brown an onion, add bouillon, and simmer for 45 minutes. Add grated carrot, white wine, and currants. After 10 minutes, mix in chopped parsley, Dijon mustard, whole grain mustard, and crème fraîche. Goes well with all kinds of stuffed dolphinfish.

... with bolete and parsley
Soak 1 oz (25 g) dried bolete. Brown lightly in 1 tablespoon butter together with 1 crushed garlic clove and chopped parsley. Stir in 2 tablespoons breadcrumbs, pepper, salt, and 1 egg. Stuff the fish with the mixture, transfer to an ovenproof dish, and drizzle with oil. Add 3 sprigs rosemary and 1 chopped garlic clove. Bake at 350 °F/180 °C. Baste with 4 tablespoons white wine after 15 minutes of cooking.

.. with tomatoes, eggplant, and basil
Lightly brown 2 chopped onions and 1 diced eggplant in oil. Add 8 peeled, diced tomatoes and cook for 10 minutes. Season with salt and pepper. Stir in 1 bunch chopped basil. Stuff the fish with the mixture, close up, transfer to a baking sheet, brush with oil, and bake for 20 minutes at 400 °F/200 °C.

RED SNAPPER
with a nut crust

Serves 4

4	red snapper fillets, skin on, ready to cook
	Salt
	Pepper
2	tomatoes, roughly chopped
/₂ bunch	scallions, cut into rings
/₂ bunch	parsley, finely chopped
5 tbsp	olive oil
/₃ cup (80 g)	butter
1 ¹/₂ cups (120 g)	hazelnuts, coarsely ground
4 sprigs	mint, finely chopped
1 ²/₃ cups (400 ml)	fish bouillon
1 ²/₃ cups (400 ml)	coconut milk

Step by step

Rinse the red snapper fillets under cold running water and pat dry. Rub with salt and pepper.

Spread the nut mixture over the red snapper. Pour over half the fish bouillon. Bake for about 25 minutes at 400 °F/200 °C.

Mix the tomatoes with the scallions, parsley, and olive oil, transfer to an ovenproof dish, and put the fish on top.

Bring the remaining fish bouillon to a boil with the coconut milk. Remove the fish and tomatoes from the dish.

Mix the softened butter, nuts, mint, salt, and pepper to a smooth paste.

Strain the cooking liquid, add to the coconut milk mixture, and serve with the fish.

COCONUT MILK INFO

Coconut milk here does not mean the liquid found in unripe coconuts, which makes a pleasant drink. Instead, it means something produced from freshly grated coconut and water. The

grated coconut is soaked and squeezed, and the resulting liquid is the coconut milk, which can be bought in stores in both sweetened and unsweetened form. In cooking, people mostly use unsweetened coconut milk.

HAZELNUT INFO

Back in the Stone Age, **hazelnuts** were already a significant part of the diet. The trees have also been the object of worship among many peoples and were said to have magic powers—hazel twigs are still used as water divining rods today. In ancient Rome, the tree was the symbol of peace. Still a favorite among chefs today, hazelnuts go particularly well with coffee or chocolate and thus often feature in desserts and pastries. The nut of the

cultivated (as opposed to wild) hazel tree is known as a filbert; it is larger, but its flavor is not so intense. Both types of nut should have the skin removed before using.

SIDE DISHES
for red snapper

All kinds of rice dishes are perfect with red snapper.

Curry and cilantro rice
Sweat 1¹/₄ cups (250 g) long-grain rice in butter with some curry powder, pour over generous 2¹/₂ cups (625 ml) water, season with salt, and simmer over low heat for 20 minutes. Fluff with a fork to let the steam escape. Stir in butter flakes and chopped cilantro.

Herb rice
Sweat 1¹/₄ cups (250 g) long-grain rice in butter with some dried herbs, pour over generous 2¹/₂ cups (625 ml) water, season with salt, and simmer over low heat for 20 minutes. Fluff with a fork and stir in butter flakes and chopped fresh herbs of your choice.

Jasmine rice
Before cooking, swirl 1¹/₄ cups (250 g) aromatic rice by hand in plenty of cold water, to prevent it from sticking. Drain in a sieve, add to generous 2¹/₂ cups (625 ml) boiling salt water, and simmer for 15–20 minutes.

... on a bed of zucchini and tomatoes
Sweat 2 diced shallots and 1 crushed garlic clove until transparent. Simmer for 10 minutes with 2 diced zucchini, 1 diced chile, and 1 teaspoon thyme. Add 5 diced tomatoes, simmer for a further 5 minutes, and season with salt and pepper. Score the skins of 4 red snapper fillets in a diamond pattern. Fry in oil, skin side down, for 5 minutes, then turn and cook for a further 5–10 minutes.

... with orange
Mix the rind and juice of 1 orange with 1 chopped onion. Marinate 4 red snapper fillets in this mixture for 30 minutes in a covered bowl. Lay the fillets side by side, skin side down, in an ovenproof dish, and season with nutmeg and pepper. Cook for 10 minutes at 400 °F/200 °C, basting occasionally with the marinade.

RED SNAPPER
several variations

Red snapper has firm white flesh that quickly dries out during cooking, so these sauce variations are perfect with it.

.. in honey and mustard sauce

Lightly brown 3 crushed garlic cloves in 1¹/₃ cups (300 g) butter. Remove from the heat and add 2 tablespoons honey, 1 tablespoon each French and whole grain mustard, pepper, and chile powder. Drizzle 4 red snapper fillets with the juice of 1 lemon and place in an ovenproof dish, skin side down. Pour the butter over the fish and bake for 15–20 minutes at 400 °F/200 °C. Sprinkle ¹/₂ bunch chopped dill over the fish to serve.

... with cauliflower and bean curry

Sweat 1 chopped onion and 3 crushed garlic cloves. Add 1²/₃ cups (400 ml) coconut milk, generous ³/₄ cup (200 ml) bouillon, 2 teaspoons sugar, and 5 tablespoons fish masala, and reduce. Add generous 1 lb (500 g) cauliflower and 11 oz (300 g) green beans (cooked), and simmer for 3–4 minutes. Drizzle 4 red snapper fillets with lemon juice and season with salt. Toss in a mixture of flour, fish masala, chile powder, and salt. Brown briefly and cook gently until tender.

.. with bean sprouts and cherry tomatoes

Brown the rings of 2 onions with generous 1 lb (500 g) bean sprouts and season with lemon juice, sugar, pepper, and salt. Cook 12 cherry tomatoes with 3 tablespoons olive oil and 1 garlic clove for 20 minutes. Brown 4 red snapper fillets fiercely in oil with 3 sprigs each thyme and rosemary and 2 garlic cloves, cook gently for 5–10 minutes until tender, and season with salt and pepper.

... with lime and curry sauce

Sweat 1 finely chopped onion with 1 sliced lime and 1 teaspoon curry powder. Pour over 3¹/₂ tablespoons (50 ml) white wine and ²/₃ cup (150 ml) fish bouillon, and reduce. Add 4 red snapper fillets, salt, and pepper. Cover and cook for 10 minutes. Mix 11 oz (300 g) cooked rice with 3¹/₂ oz (100 g) cooked lentils and season with salt and pepper. Serve the fish with rice and sauce.

99

HALIBUT
with celery and mushrooms

Serves 4

3 lb (1.4 kg)	*halibut, ready to cook, without skin*
	Lemon juice
	Salt
	Pepper
6 tbsp	*butter*
3¹/₂ oz (100 g)	*shallots, diced*
1	*stalk celery, diced*
2 tbsp	*parsley, chopped*
1³/₄ oz 50 g	*mushrooms, chopped*
¹/₂ cup (125 ml)	*white wine*
	Cayenne
3 tbsp	*crème fraîche*

INFO

Celery has become increasingly popular in recent years. Celeriac is the root of a specially bred celery plant—also known as celery root and celery knob—while the fleshy stalks of celery we enjoy in salads, dips, and vegetable dishes are traditionally blanched by heaping the earth up around them. Two common varieties are Pascal (pale green) and golden (creamy white). Incidentally, it develops its full flavor after the first frost.

Step by step

Wash the fish and slit it either side of the central bone. Drizzle with lemon juice, leave to draw, and season with salt and pepper.

Melt 3 tablespoons of butter in an oven-proof dish and lightly brown the shallots, celery, parsley, and mushrooms.

Add the fish, coat it all over in the vegetable mixture, and top with 3 tablespoons butter flakes.

Add white wine, cover the dish with aluminum foil, and bake in the oven for 10 minutes at 400 °F/200 °C.

Remove the foil, baste the fish with the cooking juices, and continue baking, uncovered, for a further 20 minutes.

Strain the sauce, season with cayenne, and stir in crème fraîche.

INFO

Over 500 varieties of **bean** are grown worldwide; fresh ones are obtainable from early summer through fall. There is a basic distinction between those that grow low to the ground and climbing beans that grow up supports, e.g. runner beans. When buying green beans, also known as fresh beans and string beans, check that they are crisp and firm, as the whole pod is edible. Versatile beans that are shelled before use include lima and fava beans. Remember also to remove the tough outer skin from individual fava beans.

Side dish

Freshly harvested beans, such as substantial **fava beans**, are a delicious accompaniment for fried or baked fish. Lightly brown 1³/₄ lb (750 g) fava beans in 1 tablespoon oil with 3¹/₂ oz (100 g) diced bacon. Pour over a little water and add salt, pepper, and a few sprigs of savory. Cover and cook for 15–20 minutes over low to medium heat.

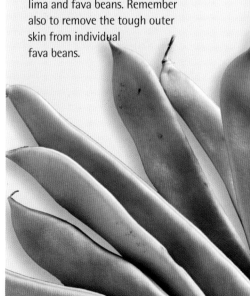

SAUCES
for halibut

Fresh with tomatoes and Feta, tangy with rosemary and shallots, or filling with bacon and gherkins, these sauces go well with halibut.

Bacon and gherkin sauce

Fry diced onion and bacon until golden brown, remove from the heat, and mix in chopped, pickled gherkins. Add mustard, crème fraîche, port, salt, and pepper. Goes well with the halibut with potatoes, celery, bell peppers and olives, and tomatoes and Feta recipe variations.

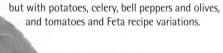

Tomato sauce

Sweat finely chopped onions and crushed garlic. Add diced tomatoes, season with basil, thyme, and rosemary, and simmer for 20 minutes. Goes well with the halibut with potatoes, celery, bell peppers and olives, and tomatoes and Feta variations.

Rosemary and shallot sauce

Lightly brown diced shallots in butter with a sprig of rosemary. Cover with red wine and reduce almost completely. Cover with fish bouillon and reduce again. Stir in small knobs of ice-cold butter. Goes well with the halibut with celery, potatoes, bell peppers and olives, and tomatoes and Feta recipe variations.

HALIBUT
severa

Here are a few variations that show how versatile halibut can be. It can be baked in the oven on a bed of vegetables; coated in flour and cooked in the oven in an open dish; browned, covered with tasty ingredients, and then baked; or stuffed and baked in the oven. You will most likely have your own ideas,

... with bell pepper, onions, and olives

Sweat strips of 2 red and 1 yellow bell peppers and 1 onion sliced into rings for 10 minutes. Add 1 tablespoon balsamic vinegar, 1 teaspoon herbes de Provence, and 3 oz (80 g) pitted black olives. Simmer, season with salt and pepper, and stir in 3 tablespoons chopped parsley. Spread over the base of an ovenproof dish. Brush the fish with 1 tablespoon oil, season with salt and pepper, arrange on the vegetables, and bake for 20 minutes.

... with tomatoes, scallions, and Feta

Coat the fish in 2 tablespoons flour, brown on both sides, and transfer to an ovenproof dish. Sweat 7 oz (200 g) scallions, cut into rings, in oil, add 3 crushed garlic cloves, 3 diced beefsteak tomatoes, 1 teaspoon dill tips, and 1 crushed bay leaf, and season with salt and pepper. Spread over the fish, sprinkle with $5\frac{1}{2}$ oz (150 g) crumbled Feta, and bake for 20 minutes at 400 °F/200 °C.

ariations

too! Halibut is best served accompanied by rice or noodles, and one of the sauces on the left. Experiment to find out which of the suggested sauces goes best with each of the preparation methods.

... with orange juice and parsley

Rub the halibut with 2 crushed garlic cloves and sprinkle with 1 bunch chopped parsley, salt, and pepper. Drizzle with 4 table-spoons oil, and coat in 4 cups (200 g) dried breadcrumbs. Transfer the fish to an ovenproof dish, pour over 2 scant cups (400 ml) freshly squeezed orange juice, dot with 3$^1/_2$ oz (100 g) butter flakes, and cover with aluminum foil. Cook for 20 minutes at 400 °F/200 °C.

... with potatoes, cherry tomatoes, and herbs

Rub the fish with lemon juice, salt, and pepper. Stuff with 1 sprig rosemary, $^1/_2$ bunch thyme, and basil. Transfer to a roasting pan. Surround the fish with 1$^3/_4$ lb (750 g) potatoes, halved and oiled, generous 1 lb (500 g) chopped cherry tomatoes, and 1 sliced lemon. Season with salt and pepper. Drizzle with 7 tablepoons olive oil. Bake for 20 minutes at 400 °F/200 °C.

SALTWATER FISH

SIDE DISHES
for halibut

Rice always goes well with fish, especially white fish such as halibut. Here are three variations:

Broccoli rice

Sweat 1$^1/_4$ cup (250 g) long-grain rice in butter. Pour over generous 2$^1/_2$ cups (625 ml) water or vegetable bouillon, season with salt, and simmer over low heat for 20 minutes. Fluff with a fork to let the steam escape then stir in broccoli florets, cooked al dente, and grated Gouda.

Viennese rice

Sweat 1$^1/_4$ cup (250 g) long-grain rice in butter. Pour over generous 2$^1/_2$ cups (625 ml) water, season with salt, add 1 onion stuck with cloves, and simmer over low heat for 20 minutes. Remove the onion, fluff the rice with a fork to let the steam escape, and stir in flakes of butter.

Turmeric rice

Sweat 1$^1/_4$ cup (250 g) long-grain rice in butter until transparent. Add turmeric, pour over generous 2$^1/_2$ cups (625 ml) water, season with salt, and simmer over low heat for 20 minutes. Fluff with a fork to let the steam escape and stir in flakes of butter.

103

TURBOT
in root vegetable and Riesling stock

INFO

Carrots are available all year round, but young baby carrots are only found in the spring. A member of the parsley family, the carrot did not acquire its typical orange color until the nineteenth century. Before that, the vegetables now known as carrots were yellow, hard, and very woody inside, so they were not very popular. Nowadays, carrots are an indispensable ingredient in a wide variety of dishes, including stews, soups, casseroles, and salads. Incidentally, in order to make the fat-soluble beta carotene easier to absorb, carrots should always be cooked with a little fat.

Serves 4

1³/₄ lb (800 g)	turbot fillets
2 cups (500 ml)	Riesling
2 tbsp	white wine vinegar
1	carrot, in thin strips
1³/₄ oz (50 g)	celeriac, in thin strips
1	onion
1	bunch mixed herbs (bay leaf, parsley, dill, and chervil)
	Salt
	Pepper
2 tbsp	butter
1 tbsp	parsley, chopped

Step by step

Skin the turbot fillets, cut into equal pieces, wash under running water, and pat dry with paper towels.

In a pot, bring a generous $^3/_4$ cup (200 ml) water to a boil with the wine and vinegar. Add the vegetables and herbs and boil for 2 minutes. Allow to cool.

Season the fish fillets with salt and pepper and add to the vegetables. Cover the pot with aluminum foil.

Put the pot in the oven for 6–8 minutes at 175 °F/80 °C.

Remove the fillets and vegetables from the stock, toss the vegetables in butter, sprinkle with parsley, and serve with the fish.

Salad

Endive is easy to prepare. Cut a head of endive into thin strips, and soak briefly in warm water to draw out the bitter substances. Dry the endive in a salad spinner. For the dressing, mix 1 small diced onion with 3 tablespoons oil, 2 tablespoons vinegar, 1 pinch sugar, salt, and pepper. Mix into the endive and serve.

Side dish

Boiled **rice** or egg noodles go best with white wine sauces and subtly flavored fish, because they do not have a dominant flavor of their own. Just put $1^1/_4$ cups (250 g) rice with double the quantity of water and a little salt in a pan, bring briefly to a boil, then simmer gently for 15–20 minutes until the rice has absorbed all the water.

TURBOT
several variations

Here, turbot fillets are cooked in a delicate stock to bring out the flavors of the fish. Simply exquisite!

... in white wine and saffron stock

Simmer the fish bones and 1 pack coarsely chopped green vegetables with 4 cups (1 liter) water for 20 minutes, strain, and reduce the stock to about 1 cup (250 ml). Poach the fish fillets in this for about 5 minutes, remove, and keep warm. Dissolve 1 teaspoon saffron in the stock, add 2 tablespoons crème fraîche, $3^1/_2$ tablespoons (50 ml) white wine, and season with salt and pepper. Serve with the fish.

... in sorrel stock

Brown 2 diced shallots. Add strips of sorrel to the pan and fry for 3 minutes. Add $^1/_2$ cup (125 ml) fish bouillon and $^1/_2$ cup (125 ml) white wine. Bring to a boil, then reduce the heat. Add the turbot fillets and poach for 5 minutes, then remove from the pan. Bring the sorrel stock to a boil, add generous $^3/_4$ cup (200 ml) light cream, reduce, and season with salt and pepper. Serve the fish with the sauce, sprinkled with finely chopped sorrel.

... in lemongrass and chile stock

Bring $1^1/_4$ cups (300 ml) fish bouillon, 7 tbsp (100 ml) white wine, 1 lemongrass stalk, 1 bay leaf, 1 chopped chile, 1 sliced lime, and 1 crushed garlic clove to a boil, then simmer gently for 15 minutes. Warm the fish fillets through in the stock for 3–5 minutes, then remove from the pan. Reduce the stock and strain. Melt 2 tbsp butter with 1 tbsp mustard, add 2 tbsp light cream and 7 tbsp (100 ml) of the strained stock, bring to a boil, season with salt and pepper, and stir in 1 egg yolk.

... in potato stock with dill cream

Reduce $1^2/_3$ cups (400 ml) fish bouillon by one-third. Simmer 1 diced onion and 7 oz (200 g) diced mealy potatoes in the stock for 12 minutes. Add the fish, cover, poach over low heat for 5–7 minutes, and remove from the pan. Purée the potatoes with stock, bring to a boil, stir in 1 bunch chopped dill and 2 tablespoons sour cream, and season with salt and pepper.

SIDE DISHES
for turbot

Various kinds of rice are a favorite with turbot. Curry and cilantro rice, or lemon rice, are especially good with fish in oriental and tart spice mixtures.

Curry and cilantro rice

Sweat 1 1/4 cups (250 g) long-grain rice in curry powder and butter, pour over double the quantity of liquid, season with salt, and simmer over low heat for 20 minutes. Fluff with a fork to let the steam escape and stir in butter flakes followed by chopped cilantro.

Tomato pilaf

Lightly brown 1 chopped onion in oil. Sweat 1 1/4 cups (250 g) rice with the onion. Add bouillon and 7 oz (200 g) peeled, diced tomatoes and cook until tender. Fold in chopped basil, salt, pepper, and butter flakes.

Lemon rice

Cook 1 1/4 cups (250 g) long-grain rice al dente with twice the quantity of water, plus salt and a bay leaf. Add finely chopped lemon balm and grated lemon peel.

.. in lemon stock with horseradish

Bring the juice of 2 lemons to a boil with 3 1/4 cups (750 ml) water, 1 onion in segments, 1 sliced carrot, and 2 bay leaves. Add the fish and poach for 4 minutes, then remove from the pan. Brown 3 tablespoons flour in 3 tablespoons butter, and pour over generous 1 1/2 cups (375 ml) strained stock. Bring to a boil with 7 tablespoons (100 ml) light cream and 2 tablespoons grated horseradish. Enrich with 2 tablespoons white wine, and season with salt and pepper.

.. in lime and sparkling wine stock

Drizzle the fish fillets with the juice of 2 limes and season with salt and pepper. Brown 2 finely chopped shallots in butter. Pour over 1 cup (250 ml) sparkling wine and reduce. Add 1 cup (250 ml) light cream and reduce a little. Add the fish fillets to the hot sauce, cover, and poach for 4–6 minutes. Finish with thyme.

PLAICE
with shrimp

Serves 4

4¹/₂ oz (125 g)	bacon, diced
2 tbsp	oil
5¹/₂ oz (150 g)	shrimp, shelled
4	plaice (each about 11 oz/300 g)
	Salt
	Pepper
1	lemon (juice of)
4 tbsp	flour
3 tbsp	butter

Step by step

Render the diced bacon slowly in the oil and fry until crisp. Remove from the pan.

Fry the plaice in the bacon fat for 5 minutes each side. Remove from the pan.

Wash the shrimp, pat dry with paper towels, and heat in the bacon fat. Remove from the pan.

Heat the butter in the pan until it bubbles, and reheat the bacon and shrimp in it.

Wash the plaice, pat dry with paper towels, season with salt and pepper, drizzle with lemon juice, and coat in the flour.

Pour the butter with shrimp and bacon over the plaice and serve immediately.

SHRIMP INFO

"Shrimp" is the generic term for this delicately flavored crustacean that is found worldwide and belongs to the

same family as the crab. Shrimp are categorized according to size—from jumbo through medium to miniature—and come in several varieties, usually distinguished by shell color: brown, pink, white, etc. Prawns are shrimplike, but have a narrower body and longer legs. Shrimp and prawns are usually eaten "peeled;" that is, they have to be removed from their shell. To do this, twist off the head and pull the shell away from the tail.

BACON INFO

Bacon is a versatile meat, which can be enjoyed at any time of the day: for instance, fried with

eggs for breakfast, broiled in a sandwich with lettuce and tomato (BLT) for a light lunch, or as a flavorful ingredient in a hearty supper of casserole or soup. Cut from either the sides or belly of a pig, which determines the amount of fat running through it, bacon is available salted and/or smoked, and either sliced into rashers of varying thickness or in a slab.

SALTWATER FISH

SAUCES
for plaice

The classic sauce to accompany fish is dill sauce. Bell pepper and vermouth, or orange-flavor sauces, are a little more unusual.

Dill sauce
Mix together sour cream, crème fraîche, finely chopped dill, salt, pepper, lemon juice, and mustard. Goes well with plaice with shrimp, ham and Emmental, and the potato and vegetable, sesame crumb, and almond coating variations.

Orange cream sauce
Bring orange juice to a boil and season with cayenne. Add light cream and bind with ice-cold butter flakes. Goes well with the plaice with potato and vegetable, sesame crumb, and almond coating variations.

Bell pepper and vermouth sauce
Sweat finely chopped onion and crushed garlic. Add roughly chopped bell pepper. Simmer in vermouth, bouillon, and light cream, then purée and season with salt and pepper. Goes well with plaice with tomatoes and anchovies, ham and Emmental, and the potato and vegetable, sesame crumb, and almond coatings.

... with tomatoes, anchovies, and olives
Sweat 1 finely chopped onion and 1 crushed garlic clove until transparent. Add generous 1lb (500 g) diced tomatoes, $1^3/_4$ oz (50 g) pitted and quartered olives, and $^3/_4$ oz (20 g) anchovy fillets. Season with salt, pepper, and 1 bunch chopped parsley. Season the plaice with salt and pepper and coat in flour. Fry in 4 tablespoons clarified butter for 5 minutes each side. Serve with the tomato mixture and lemon segments.

... with a sesame crumb coating
Beat 2 eggs and mix with 2 tablespoons light cream. Mix together 3 cups (150 g) dried breadcrumbs, 5 tablespoons parsley, and 3 tablespoons sesame seeds. Flour the plaice, dip in the egg mixture, and coat in the sesame crumb. Fry for 5 minutes on each side. Drain on paper towels. Keep warm in the oven.

PLAICE
several variations

Because of its flat shape, plaice is perfect—whether with or without a coating, stuffed or plain, fried or baked. However you choose to prepare it, plaice will always taste good.

... with boiled ham and Emmental

Slice $3^1/_2$ oz (100 g) each boiled ham and Emmental. Open out whole, boned plaice, cover the bottom half with ham, cheese, and chopped parsley, fold over, secure with toothpicks, and season with salt and pepper. Coat the fish first in 1 tablespoon flour, then in 1 beaten egg, and then in 4 tablespoons dried breadcrumbs. Fry in oil for 5 minutes each side.

... with a potato and vegetable coating

Cut 7 oz (200 g) carrots and $^1/_2$ leek in thin strips and boil in salt water. Season the plaice with salt and pepper and drizzle with lemon juice. Mix 9 oz (250 g) finely grated potatoes with the cooked vegetables, 1 egg, and 3 tablespoons flour, and season with salt and pepper. Coat the fish in this mixture and deep fry in hot fat for 5–10 minutes until golden brown.

... with pesto and pecorino

Season the fish with salt and pepper. Brown on both sides in butter, then transfer to an ovenproof dish. Mix $5^1/_2$ oz (150 g) pesto with 6 tablespoons (40 g) pecorino and spread evenly over the fillets. Bake for 5–6 minutes at 400 °F/200 °C.

... with an almond coating

Rub the plaice with the juice of 2 lemons, and season with salt and pepper. Toss in 7 oz (200 g) ground almonds and fry for 5 minutes each side over medium heat.

COOKING FISH INFO

By the way: **flatfish**, which category includes plaice, have a dark top skin; when they are

poached, they tend to be cooked in the liquid lighter side up, but served dark side up. Presumably it is because the fish just look better when presented this way.

POTATOES INFO

Potatoes in stores are generally divided into two different types by their consistency when cooked: waxy (firm) and mealy (soft). Firm potatoes are used for fries, gratins, and potato salad,

because it is important that the potatoes do not fall apart. Small, new waxy potatoes can be cooked and eaten in their skins. The mealy varieties are suitable for stews and mash; the large "baker" type is perfect for cooking in its skin in the oven.

Serves 4

1	*Savoy cabbage*
7 oz (200 g)	*salmon fillet*
3 tbsp	*lemon juice*
	Salt
	Pepper
1¹/₃ cups (150 g)	*crème fraîche*
8 small	*plaice fillets (each about 5 oz/150 g)*
	Toothpicks
14 oz (400 g)	*potatoes, peeled and diced*
2 tbsp	*butter*
	Nutmeg

Step by step

Separate the leaves of the cabbage, blanch, and rinse in cold water. Set 8 large leaves aside and cut the remainder into strips.

Lay the rolls on the cabbage leaves, turn in the edges and roll up. Fasten with toothpicks.

Purée the salmon. Mix with ¹/₂ tablespoon of lemon juice, salt, pepper, and 1 table-spoon of crème fraîche.

Mix together the potatoes and cabbage with the melted butter. Add the remaining crème fraîche and 3–4 tablespoons water, and season with nutmeg.

Rinse the plaice fillets, pat dry, and drizzle with the remaining lemon juice. Spread with the salmon purée and roll up.

Lay the cabbage and plaice rolls on the potato mixture. Cover and fry gently for 20–25 minutes over medium heat.

PLAICE ROLLS
with Savoy cabbage and salmon

SAUCES
for plaice rolls

Now we just need a tasty sauce to go with the plaice rolls, and the dish will be perfect! Here are a couple with a hint of the Orient:

Vegetable, horseradish, and caper sauce
Dust diced carrots, potatoes, and onions with flour, brown lightly, and cook in bouillon. Add cream and grated horseradish, bring to a boil, season with salt and pepper, and add capers and chopped dill. Goes well with the plaice rolls with Savoy cabbage and salmon, herby cream cheese, eggplant and bell pepper, and kohlrabi and parsley variations.

Curry and cream sauce
Sauté diced onion. Pour over fish bouillon and white wine, and reduce a little. Stir in crème fraîche. Beat a little sauce together with egg yolk, curry powder, salt, and pepper, and add to the sauce. Goes well with the plaice rolls with Savoy cabbage and salmon, herby cream cheese, eggplant and bell pepper, and spinach and leek variations.

PLAICE ROLLS
severa

Flatfish fillets are perfect for roulades. Not only do they look attractive, they also give you the chance to spread the fillets beforehand with spicy pastes, or cover them with other tasty ingredients and herbs. Be sure to use flat ingredients or those that can be cut into flat strips, such as leeks.

... with herby cream cheese and cherry tomatoes
Form rolls of marinated plaice. Place them in layers in an oven-proof dish. Make crosswise cuts in 8 cherry tomatoes and insert them between the rolls. Cut 4 oz (120 g) cream cheese with herbs into small pieces, and place on top of the fish rolls. Pour over 5 tablespoons white wine and 4 tablespoons light cream, and cook in the oven for 20 minutes at 350 °F/180 °C. Sprinkle with chopped parsley.

... with spinach, currants, and leeks
Spread strips of leek over the marinated fish. Roll up and fasten. Sweat 1 finely chopped onion and 1 crushed garlic clove until transparent. Brown the plaice rolls in the onion and garlic then remove from the pan. Sweat 1 lb (450 g) frozen spinach in the same pan and add 2 tablespoons currants. Season with salt, pepper, and nutmeg. Arrange the fish rolls on top, and put a little crème fraîche on each. Steam for 5 minutes.

ariations

Then simply roll up and either bake in the oven, or fry gently in a skillet.

SAUCES
for plaice rolls

Here are a couple of tasty ideas for sauces to go with plaice rolls, which add a bit of pep with shrimp, capers, or horseradish.

... with eggplant, bell pepper, and zucchini

Sweat 1 onion, sliced into rings, and 1 crushed garlic clove with 2 each diced eggplant, zucchini, and bell peppers. Simmer in $^1/_2$ cup (125 ml) bouillon, and season with salt, pepper, and 4 tablespoons Italian herbs. Transfer to an ovenproof dish. Brush the fish with 2 tablespoons pesto, roll up, and arrange on the vegetables. Sprinkle with grated Parmesan, and bake for 20 minutes at 350 °F/180 °C.

Herb butter sauce

Heat 2 tablespoons herb butter, and make a roux with flour or cornstarch. Pour over milk, add a bay leaf, and simmer for about 5 minutes. Season with salt and nutmeg. Goes well with all recipe variations.

.. with kohlrabi and parsley

Sprinkle marinated fish fillets with 1 tablespoon chopped parsley, roll up, and fasten with a toothpick. Lightly brown 1 finely chopped onion and 2 thinly sliced kohlrabi in butter. Add 4 tablespoons white wine and simmer for 5 minutes. Stir in1 tablespoon crème fraîche, arrange the fish rolls on top, and sprinkle with chopped kohlrabi leaves. Cover and cook for 5–7 minutes.

Mushroom and shrimp sauce

Sweat sliced mushrooms with chopped onion. Dust with flour, pour over light cream, and bring to a boil. Add shrimp and fish stock. Season with salt, pepper, sugar, and Worcestershire sauce. Goes well with the plaice rolls with Savoy cabbage and salmon, herby cream cheese, eggplant and bell pepper, and kohlrabi and parsley variations.

FILLETS OF SOLE
with chervil and Riesling

INFO

Cream is the fatty component that settles on top of untreated milk. Because of the homogenization process, however, during which the fat globules are broken down and dispersed, this no longer happens. Cream is produced by centrifugation. What is left is low-fat milk. To be called cream, it has to have a milkfat content of at least 18%. Light cream has a milkfat content of 18–30%, and heavy cream a milkfat content of 36–40%. Light whipping cream falls between these two, with a milkfat content of 30–36%. It is particularly versatile in cooking.

Serves 4

11 oz (300 g)	sole fillets
1	lemon (juice of)
1	shallot, finely chopped
²/₃ cup (150 ml)	fish bouillon (bottled)
3¹/₂ tbsp (50 ml)	Riesling
7 tbsp (100 ml)	light cream
2 tbsp	butter
	Salt
	Pepper
2 tbsp	chervil, finely chopped

Step by step

Wash the sole fillets, pat dry with paper towels, and drizzle with half the lemon juice.

Bring the diced shallot to a boil with the fish bouillon and Riesling, and reduce by two-thirds. Strain the stock into a pan.

Add the sole fillets to the stock, cover, and cook for 2 minutes. Remove from the pan and keep warm.

Add the cream to the stock and reduce until smooth. Beat in knobs of cold butter.

Season with salt, pepper, and the remaining lemon juice. Sprinkle with chopped chervil and serve immediately.

Side dish

The refined flavor of sole needs a worthy accompaniment, and **almond broccoli** is just right. Blanch generous 1 lb (500 g) broccoli florets in salt water, then coat in 2 tablespoons warmed, clarified butter and fry gently.

Season with salt and pepper and remove from the pan. Add a little more clarified butter to the pan, caramelize 1 tablespoon sugar, and pour over a little water. Add the broccoli and stir in 3 tablespoons slivered almonds.

Side dish

Make your own **ribbon noodles**. You do not need a pasta machine, but it does take a bit of time. Mix $3^1/_4$ cups (500 g) wheat flour with 4 eggs and 4 egg yolks, 2 tablespoons olive oil, and a little salt. Knead the dough until smooth, and leave to rest for 30 minutes. Roll out on a floured worktop,

and set aside for another 30 minutes. Cut into broad strips about $2^1/_2$ in. (6 cm) in width. Then cut into smaller strips $^1/_2$–$^3/_4$ in. (1.5–2 cm) wide and allow to dry before cooking.

SOLE FILLETS
several variations

If you want to serve something really special one day, cook a sole! Its delicate white flesh is full of flavor. Prepare the sole in whole fillets, accompanied by a delicate sauce that emphasizes its refined taste.

... with shrimp and mushrooms

Cook the sole with 1 tablespoon melted butter, the liquid from 1 can shrimp, and $^1/_2$ cup (125 ml) white wine for 10 minutes at 440 °F/225 °C. Pour off the liquid and keep the sole warm. Thicken the cooking liquid in a pan with $^1/_2$ cup (125 ml) sour cream, add salt, pepper, and 10 pitted olives, and simmer. Arrange $1^1/_4$ lb (600 g) cooked and mashed potato, 7 oz (200 g) sautéed, sliced mushrooms, and the shrimp on a plate around the sole. Serve immediately with the sauce.

... with spinach and white wine

Simmer the fish bones with chopped casserole vegetables, pepper, salt, thyme, 1 bay leaf, 1 cup (250 ml) white wine, and $1^1/_4$ cups (300 ml) water for 30 minutes. Strain. Add 1 cup (250 ml) milk, reduce, and thicken. Sweat 7 oz (200 g) chopped spinach, season, and transfer to an ovenproof dish. Brown the fish, season with salt and pepper, and arrange on the spinach. Mix the pan juices with 4 tbsp vermouth and stir into the sauce. Cover the fish with the sauce and 3 tbsp grated Parmesan, dot with butter, and bake for 15–20 minutes.

... with zucchini, tomatoes, and olives

Lightly brown 3 finely chopped shallots and 2 crushed garlic cloves with 1 sliced zucchini and 2 chopped scallions. Add 14 oz (400 g) canned tomatoes, black and green pitted olives, and 2 tablespoons freshly chopped basil, and season with salt and pepper. Simmer for 10 minutes. Put the fish and the sauce in an ovenproof dish. Sprinkle with 6 tablespoons grated Parmesan and bake for 15–20 minutes at 400 °F/200 °C.

... with rhubarb and asparagus tips

Melt 8 teaspoons brown sugar, pour over 7 tablespoons (100 ml) orange juice, and flavor with vanilla, cinnamon, and anise. Cook $1^1/_4$ lb (600 g) diced rhubarb in the mixture and purée. Then cook 7 oz (200 g) rhubarb stalks gently in the purée. Fold in generous 1 lb (500 g) cooked asparagus tips. Reduce generous $^3/_4$ cup (200 ml) vegetable bouillon, add 1 teaspoon sherry vinegar, and thicken with butter. Stir into the rhubarb sauce, add the fish, and bake for 30 minutes at 250 °F/120 °C.

... with lime and chive butter

Mix 7 tablespoons (100 g) butter with the juice of 1 lime, grated rind of $^1/_2$ lime, and $^1/_2$ bunch chopped chives. Spread between pairs of fish fillets. Drizzle 3 tablespoons melted butter over the fish. Mix 2 tablespoons dried breadcrumbs with the grated rind of $^1/_2$ lime, and sprinkle over the fish. Bake for 25 minutes at 350 °F/180 °C.

... with eggplant and basil butter

Sweat $^1/_2$ diced eggplant with 1 each diced onion, zucchini, red bell pepper, and yellow bell pepper. Add 1 chopped tomato, simmer for 5 minutes, and season with salt and pepper. Fry the fish briefly. Purée 2 bunches basil with 5 tablespoons Noilly Prat and 7 tablespoons (100 g) softened butter. Season with salt and pepper, add to the fish pan juices, and heat until frothy. Add 3 tablespoons light cream. Serve with the vegetables and fish.

SIDE DISHES
for sole fillets

Potatoes go well with the delicate flesh of sole fillets. Here are three variations, some tossed in butter, and some fried.

Buttered potatoes

Peel freshly boiled potatoes. Melt some butter, add a little salt, and toss the potatoes in it.

Rösti made from raw potatoes

Peel waxy potatoes, grate, and squeeze dry in a cloth. Heat oil in a pan, fry portions of grated potato on both sides until golden brown, and sprinkle with salt.

Rösti made from boiled potatoes

Peel leftover boiled potatoes, grate coarsely, and season with salt. Melt some butter in a skillet and fry the grated potato gently on one side until golden brown, pressing it into a large cake. Carefully turn the potato cake over, add some more butter to the skillet, and fry on the other side.

119

SEAFOOD

Seafood means all the delicious creatures that the sea has to offer, except for fish.

These include mussels, shrimp, lobster, crabs and other crustaceans, and also squid.

From blue mussels in sauce via shrimp kebabs to up-market lobster, in this section you will find an array of recipes, all complemented by appropriate sauces and side dishes.

BLUE MUSSELS
with crème fraîche and parsley

Serves 4

4¹/₂ lb (2 kg)	*blue mussels*
2 tbsp	*butter*
2	*shallots, finely chopped*
3 sprigs	*parsley*
1 sprig	*thyme*
1	*bay leaf*
1 cup (250 ml)	*white wine*
5 tbsp (100 g)	*crème fraîche*
	Pepper
/₂ bunch	*flat-leaf parsley, chopped*

Step by step

Scrub the mussels under running water, using a brush. Discard open mussels (see Info).

Add the mussels, cover, and cook over high heat until the shells open.

Heat the butter in a large pan and sweat the shallots for a few minutes, until transparent.

Now discard any mussels that have failed to open.

Tie the parsley and thyme sprigs and bay leaf in a bunch. Add to the pan after minutes, and pour over the wine.

Strain the mussel liquid, add the crème fraîche, bring to a boil, season with pepper, and pour over the mussels. Sprinkle with chopped parsley.

MUSSELS INFO

The old rule that you should only eat **mussels** when there is an "r" in the month—that is, from September to April—came about as follows: mussels filter their food from the water, which means that they also take in harmful substances. In summer, when water temperatures are high and there may be poisonous algae floating in the water, the level of pollutant ingestion is particularly high, making mussels inedible. Nowadays, however, the pollution controls are so strict that there is no longer any danger, even in months without an "r" in them.

Scrub **mussels** with a brush under running water, but only use those with a strong smell of sea and seaweed. Allow the mussels to drain well and discard any that are already open or have badly damaged shells. Any mussels that have not opened after cooking should also be discarded. Then remove the mussel "beard" by running a small knife along the shell.

123

SIDE DISHES
for mussels

You can simply serve bread with blue mussels. If you would like to make things more interesting, try out one of the following suggestions.

Garlic and parsley toast
Mix soft butter, salt, crushed garlic, and diced onion with a little chopped parsley. Toast white bread lightly, spread with the garlic butter, and cut in half. Bake for 10 minutes.

Garlic and herb baguette
Mix butter with finely chopped chives and parsley, a little fresh basil, and crushed garlic. Cut diagonals into a baguette without slicing right through. Spread the garlic butter in between. Wrap in aluminum foil and bake for 10–15 minutes at 400 °F/200 °C.

Buttered black bread
Slices of thickly buttered black rye bread are served with "Rheinland-style" mussels, but also go well with mussels prepared in other ways.

BLUE MUSSELS
severa

Common or blue mussels are among the most popular mussel varieties, possibly because, unlike other kinds, they are still reasonably priced. They are also very easy to prepare and come with a delightful scent of the sea. The simplest way of preparing and serving them is probably when the mussels are

... with white wine, sour cream, and curry
Cook the mussels in 1 cup (250 ml) white wine until they open, then remove the upper shells. Mix generous ³/₄ cup (200 ml) sour cream with 1 teaspoon curry powder, 1 egg yolk, salt, and pepper, pour over the mussels, and broil under moderate heat for 2–3 minutes.

... with onions, garlic, and herb butter
Sweat 4 large, finely chopped onions and 5 crushed garlic cloves in 7 tablespoons (100 g) herb butter. Add 2 leeks in thin rings, a little thyme, and 10 green peppercorns, brown lightly, and pour over 1 cup (250 ml) white wine. Add the mussels, cover, and simmer for 10–15 minutes.

...ariations

...ooked in a tasty stock with finely chopped carrots, ...eeks, and celery, and eaten with nothing more ...han bread and butter. Here, we present a couple ...f other delicious ways of cooking whole mussels in ...heir shells.

.. with tomatoes, chile, and casserole vegetables

...ightly brown 2 onions cut into rings, the diced flesh of ³/₄ lb (750 g) tomatoes, 2 crushed garlic cloves, 1 finely ...hopped chile, and 1 pack finely chopped casserole vegetables ...n 5 tablespoons oil. Add 1 sprig thyme and 2 bay leaves. Pour ...ver 1 cup (250 ml) white wine and bring to a boil. Add the ...ussels, and cook with the lid on.

.. with bell pepper and coconut milk

...weat 1 red bell pepper in strips, 2 finely chopped chiles, ...finely chopped onions, and 2 crushed garlic cloves. Sprinkle ...ith 1 teaspoon each curry powder and paprika, and a pinch ...ach coriander and cumin, pour over generous ³/₄ cup (200 ml) ...oconut milk, and bring to a boil. Flavor with the juice of ...₂ lime and cayenne. Cook the mussels in the mixture.

DRINKS
for blue mussels

Light white wines or a good beer go well with blue mussel variations.

White wine

Pescador Blanc is a fresh, slightly sparkling Spanish white wine. It goes well with all mussel dishes.

Beer

A strong Pilsner goes well with mussels with onions, garlic, and herb butter, particularly if you have chosen buttered black bread as a side dish.

White wine

Muscadet from the "Pays de la Loire-Atlantique" region tastes pleasantly mild and does not overwhelm the taste of the mussels. Goes with all mussel dishes.

SCALLOPS
INFO

Fresh **scallops** must be heavy and closed. To open, lay them with the flatter shell on top and run a knife along the edge of

the upper shell. Then fold the flat shell upward. Remove all the black innards and the beard. Only the cylindrical white muscle between the shells and the orange-red roe (coral) are used. They are considered a special delicacy.

MUSHROOMS
INFO

The best known **wild mushroom** is the common field mushroom, which is closely related to the

cultivated common-store mushroom. There is also the aromatic horse mushroom, with its subtle flavor of licorice; the parasol mushroom, with its musky taste; and the oyster mushroom, which has a peppery, oyster-like tang. As wild mushrooms tend to be seasonal, however, it is the cultivated varieties, available all year round, that serve the bulk of the market.

Serves 4

1³/₄ lb (800 g)	scallops, without shells
3¹/₄ cups (750 ml)	white wine
2	shallots, diced
5¹/₂ oz (150 g)	casserole vegetables, diced
1 tsp each	salt, pepper
3 tsp	sugar
1	bay leaf
¹/₂ tsp	peppercorns
1 sprig	thyme
6 tbsp	butter
3 tbsp	flour
7 tbsp (100 ml)	light cream
1	egg yolk
9 oz (250 g)	mushrooms, halved
2–3 tbsp	dried breadcrumbs

Step by step

Separate the flesh from the roe (coral), wash, and pat dry with paper towels.

Brown 3 tablespoons of butter with flour, pour over 1¹/₂ cups (375 ml) of the stock, and boil for 10 minutes. Add the cream, and reduce by one-third.

Boil 3¹/₄ cups (750 ml) of water. Add the wine, shallots, vegetables, and flavorings, and simmer for 20 minutes. Strain.

Season with salt and pepper. Stir the egg yolk with a little stock until smooth, and combine with the sauce without further cooking.

Cook the scallops gently in the stock for 5 minutes, adding the coral after 4 minutes. Remove from the stock and slice.

Fry the mushrooms in some butter. Arrange the scallops, sauce, breadcrumbs, and 3 tablespoons of butter flakes on the shells and broil under moderate heat.

SCALLOPS
with mushrooms and white wine

SAUCES
for scallops

Sweet and sharp flavors complement the taste of scallops particularly well. Why not try out these suggestions?

SCALLOPS
severa

With their firm, white flesh and nutty flavor, scallops are considered a real delicacy. The classic way of preparing them is au gratin, either baked in their shells, or with the flesh baked separately and then served in the shells. Looking so appetizing when served this way, scallops are pretty impressive.

Ginger and orange sauce
Sweat finely grated ginger and diced shallots until transparent, and pour over sherry vinegar. Dissolve orange jelly in the liquid and mix with ground black and red pepper. Goes well with the scallops with fennel recipe variation.

... with shallots, garlic, and chile
Sweat $3^1/_2$ oz (100 g) diced shallots, 2 crushed garlic cloves, and 1 diced chile. Add the scallop meat and coral, and season with salt and pepper. Reduce $3^1/_2$ tablespoons (50 ml) fish bouillon, stir 2 table-spoons chopped parsley into $3^1/_2$ tablespoons (50 ml) light cream reduced by one-third, and add to the sauce. Arrange on the shells, sprinkle with 2 tablespoons grated white breadcrumbs, dot with 2 tablespoons butter flakes, and broil until golden brown.

Saffron sauce
Sauté finely chopped shallots in butter, add white wine, and reduce. Stir in fish bouillon and reduce again. Add crème fraîche and dissolved saffron, and simmer until the sauce has thickened slightly.

... with potatoes, filberts, and parsley
Drizzle 4 small potatoes with olive oil, slice thinly, arrange on the scallop shells, and bake at 425 °F/220 °C. As soon as the potatoes begin to brown, arrange the scallops on top, and bake for 5 minutes. Mix together 2 tablespoons each butter and breadcrumbs, 2 teaspoons ground filberts, and chopped parsley and season with salt and pepper. Spread over the scallops and broil until golden brown.

... variations

If you only buy the scallop meat, try asking the fishmonger for a few shells as well.

SAUCES
for scallops

Simply delicious—firm, aromatic scallop flesh, combined with a tasty sauce. Here are two suggestions that go with all the variations:

... with fennel and heavy cream

Lightly brown 1 finely diced fennel. Add 1 crushed garlic clove and 1 diced shallot, and 3 tablespoons Chardonnay. Reduce, and season with salt and pepper. Beat 5 tablespoons heavy cream until almost stiff, and fold two-thirds of it into the fennel sauce. Brown the scallops. Spread the sauce on the scallop shells, top with the scallops, coral, and remaining cream, and bake at 425 °F/220 °C .

Bell pepper sauce

Reduce white wine and fish bouillon by one-half, and season with salt and pepper. Thicken with butter flakes. Boil bell peppers in salt water, drain and purée, add thyme, and beat into the wine stock until frothy.

... with raisins and capers

Beat 5 tablespoons butter to a foam and add 1 egg yolk. Stir in tablespoons breadcrumbs, 1 oz (30 g) chopped sun-dried tomatoes, and 3 tablespoons each raisins and capers. Season with 1 tablespoon lemon juice, a little sugar, salt, pepper, and teaspoon tandoori masala, and chill in the icebox. Arrange the scallops on the shells, cover with the chilled sauce, and bake for 15 minutes at 425 °F/220 °C.

Parsley sauce

Mix together vinegar, mustard, salt, pepper, and sugar, and beat in some oil. Season, and finish with finely chopped parsley.

CLAMS
with tomatoes and white wine

INFO

Olive oil comes in various qualities. The label on the bottle is crucial. Simple olive oil consists of refined (industrially produced) and native oil, and has been heat-treated. As a result, it has no vitamin content. Native olive oil is produced naturally, and contains many unhealthy saturated fatty acids. "Native olive oil extra," "cold pressed," and "extra virgin" are indications of high-quality oils. They are machine-pressed and not heated.

Serves 4

2¹/₂ lb (1.2 kg)	*clams*
1	*onion, diced*
2	*garlic cloves, finely chopped*
2 tbsp	*olive oil*
generous 1 lb (500 g)	*beefsteak tomatoes, peeled and finely chopped*
1 cup (250 ml)	*white wine*
1	*bay leaf*
1 sprig	*oregano*
1 sprig	*thyme*
	Salt
	Pepper
2 tbsp	*parsley, chopped*

Step by step

Brush the clams under cold water and soak in cold water for 2 hours. Discard any that are open.

Sweat the onion and garlic in oil until transparent. Add the beefsteak tomatoes, peeled and finely chopped.

Add the white wine and herbs. Cover and simmer for about 10 minutes over low heat, and season to taste.

Add the clams to the pan, partially cover, and cook for 10 minutes. Discard any that have not opened.

Pour the sauce over the cooked clams, sprinkle with chopped parsley, and serve immediately.

Side dish

With this dish, you can simply serve fresh, white bread or—if that seems too meager—**fried rice with onion**. Here is a variation on plain boiled rice, with flavor-enhancing onion. Sweat 9 oz cups (250 g) long-grain rice with 1 finely chopped onion until transparent. Add twice the quantity of water and bring to a boil. Simmer over low heat for 20 minutes.

Side dish

Linguine with tomato sauce: cook the linguine al dente. Sauté onion and garlic, then add bouillon and puréed tomatoes. Reduce a little, then stir in diced tomatoes with chopped thyme. Mix the linguine with the sauce.

SIDE DISHES
for clams

Different kinds of rice go beautifully with all our clam variations.

Red rice
Sweat 1¼ cups (250 g) red Camargue rice in oil with 1 chopped onion. Add twice the quantity of water, season with salt, and cook al dente.

Wild rice with bell pepper
Sweat 1¼ cups (250 g) wild rice with chopped onion. Add twice the quantity of water, season with salt, and cook al dente. Stir in 1 diced red bell pepper 10 minutes before the end of cooking time. Sprinkle with strips of basil.

Bulgur with olives
Leave 1¼ cups (250 g) bulgur to swell in twice the quantity of hot bouillon. Stir in 3½ oz (100 g) pitted, chopped black olives, and 1 tablespoon chopped thyme.

CLAMS
several

Because they cook very quickly, clams can be cooked whole in their shells in sauce. They only have to warm through in it for a few minutes. You can tell when they are ready, because the shells open. Any that have not opened must then be discarded. Here are four variations of the recipe,

... with garlic and lemon
Sauté 2 garlic cloves in 2–3 tablespoons oil until golden brown. Remove from the pan, and add ½ cup (125 ml) vegetable bouillon with 1¾ lb (800 g) drained clams. Simmer with a few cilantro leaves, shaking occasionally, until all the clams have opened. Season with a little black pepper, and drizzle with the juice of 1 lemon. Serve with lemon segments.

... with leeks and carrots
Sauté 2 leeks, cut into rings, in 3 tablespoons white wine and 7 tablespoons (100 g) butter. Add ⅔ cup (150 ml) light cream, and simmer over low heat. Cut generous 1 lb (500 g) carrots into strips, blanch, and add to the pan. Season with pepper and nutmeg. Bring generous ¾ cup (200 ml) white wine to a boil, add 2½ lb (1.2 kg) clams, and cook. When the clams have opened, add the sauce.

variations

which are flavored in very different ways—spicy with a hint of lemon, classy with leek and white wine, fiery with chile, and creamy and mild with saffron and cream.

... with chile and basil

Heat 7 tablespoons (100 ml) olive oil, then add 2 garlic cloves and 2$^1/_2$ lb (1.2 kg) clams. Cook until the clams open. Add 3 sliced chiles, 2 tablespoons chile paste, and 2 teaspoons soy sauce. Pour over 1$^1/_4$ cups (300 ml) vegetable bouillon, simmer for 3 minutes, then sprinkle with 1 handful shredded basil.

.. with saffron, cream, and parsley

Sauté 1 crushed garlic clove in 1 tablespoon oil. Add 2$^1/_2$ lb (1.2 kg) clams, and pour over $^2/_3$ cup (150 ml) white wine. Cover, then simmer until all the clams have opened. Add 1$^1/_4$ cups (300 ml) light cream, 1 sachet saffron, and pepper to the clams. Sprinkle with 1 bunch finely chopped parsley.

SEAFOOD

SIDE DISHES
for clams

Here, you can choose between garlic bread, parsley rice, and green ribbon noodles.

Garlic bread
Toast slices of baguette. Spread with finely chopped garlic cloves and herb butter. Garnish with parsley.

Parsley rice
Cook 1$^1/_4$ cups (250 g) long-grain rice in twice the quantity of salt water for 20 minutes. Drain. Stir in 3 tablespoons freshly chopped parsley.

Pasta verde with red pepper
Spinach pasta, seasoned with freshly ground red pepper after cooking, goes well with clams in saffron.

133

JUMBO SHRIMP KEBABS
with pineapple and bell pepper

Serves 4

1³/₄ lb (800 g)	jumbo shrimp, peeled
4 tbsp	oil
3 tbsp	soy sauce
3 tbsp	white rum
5¹/₂ oz (150 g)	canned pineapple chunks, with juice
1 tsp	sugar
1 tsp	ground ginger
	Salt
	Pepper
1	red bell pepper
	Wooden or metal skewers

INFO

Shrimp constitute an extensive family of crustaceans. They are categorized by size, as follows: colossal (10 or less shrimp per pound in weight); jumbo (11–15); extra larg (16–20); large (21–30); medium (31–35); small (36–45); miniature (about 100); and titi (about 400). The rock shrimp is a particularly flavorsome variety; it is large (20–25) and found off the coast of Florida, among other places.

Step by step

Slit the shrimp along the back. Remove the dark innards with the point of a knife.

Mix together the oil, soy sauce, rum, 5 tablespoons of pineapple juice, sugar, ginger, salt, and pepper.

Pour the marinade over the shrimp. Chill in the icebox for 45 minutes.

Cut the bell pepper into squares about 1¹/₄ x 1¹/₄ in. (3 x 3 cm).

Pat the shrimp dry and spear on the skewers, alternating with pieces of pineapple and bell pepper. If using wooden skewers, remember to soak them beforehand.

Either grill on a barbecue or broil for 8 minutes, brushing frequently with the marinade.

INFO

There are over a thousand different varieties of **pepper**, and of course you cannot find all of them in every store. They differ in shape, color, flavor, and pungency. The chile, also known as hot pepper, and somewhat milder sweet pepper, or peperoni, belong to the capsicum family. The bell pepper is another type of capsicum and, like the fresh chile, is usually green, red, orange, or yellow (the green is, in fact, only an unripe version of the red). All bell peppers are excellent either raw in salads or as an ingredient in cooked dishes. Another important relative is the sweetly flavored pimiento, a heart-shaped pepper from which paprika is made.

Side dish

To go with the shrimp kebabs, make **curry and pineapple rice**. First sweat 1¹/₄ cups (250 g) long-grain rice in 4 tablespoons butter until transparent. Add 1 tablespoon curry powder, pour over twice the quantity of liquid (preferably chicken bouillon), season with salt, and simmer over low heat for 20 minutes. Fluff with a fork to let the steam escape, then stir in 2 tablespoons butter flakes and 1³/₄ oz (50 g) diced pineapple.

SEAFOOD

DIPS
for shrimp

Creams and dips for shrimp kebabs should be thick enough to enable the food to be held and eaten while standing up. If made too thin and runny, the risk is having the dips run everywhere.

Aïoli

Stir egg yolk, mustard, and salt into a creamy mix. Beat in oil, a drop at a time at first, then in a thin, steady stream. Mix with crushed garlic, lemon juice, and pepper. Goes well with the basil and garlic, and cherry tomato marinade recipe variations.

Dill and sour cream dip

Mix sour cream with finely chopped onions, crushed garlic, and dill. Season well with salt and pepper. Goes well with the basil and garlic, and cherry tomato recipe variations.

Capers and anchovy cream

Purée drained capers with pine nuts, anchovy fillets, olives, finely chopped parsley, and lemon juice. Beat an egg yolk until frothy, and gradually stir in 5 tablespoons olive oil. Mix with the purée to give a sauce, and season with salt and pepper. Goes well with the basil and garlic, and cherry tomato variations.

SHRIMP KEBABS
several

Whether you cook them on the barbecue, under the broiler, or on a rack in the oven, shrimp kebabs are ready in a flash. But think about the time involved, if you want to steep the shrimp in a marinade before cooking. Shrimp kebabs are runaway favorites at any barbecue. You can, of course, prepare the kebabs

... with a basil and garlic marinade

Mix $1/2$ bunch finely chopped basil with 1 crushed garlic clove, 1 teaspoon ground paprika, olive oil, salt, and pepper. Spread over the shrimp and leave to draw. Thread onto skewers and brush with the remaining marinade. Grill, broil, or bake for 8–9 minutes, turning regularly.

... with a mango and lime marinade

Make a marinade from 2 crushed garlic cloves, the juice of 2 limes, 2 tablespoons olive oil, and a little water. Thread shrimp on skewers, alternating with 2 each diced mangoes and limes. Steep in the marinade in the icebox for at least 1 hour. Grill for 8–9 minutes, brushing frequently with the marinade.

variations

beforehand, so they are ready to cook. But it is more fun for the guests if they can put their own kebab together. Just lay out portions of various ingredients, including shrimp in 2 or 3 different marinades, and some skewers. If using wooden ones, remember to soak them in water beforehand.

... with a cherry tomato and rosemary marinade

Mix together $^1/_2$ cup (120 ml) olive oil, 3 tablespoons soy sauce, the juice of 1 lemon, salt, pepper, rosemary, and thyme. Marinate the shrimp for 2 hours in the icebox. Thread skewers alternately with shrimp and cherry tomatoes. Pour 1 tablespoon marinade over each kebab. Grill for 9 minutes.

... with shallots, and an orange and ginger marinade

Mix together the thinly peeled rind and juice of 2 oranges, $^3/_4$ oz (50 g) thinly sliced ginger, 1 tablespoon lightly crushed green peppercorns, 1 bunch cilantro leaves, and 7 tablespoons (100 ml) olive oil. Thread skewers alternately with shrimp and shallots, and steep in the marinade in the icebox. Grill for 8–9 minutes, brushing with the marinade.

SALADS
for shrimp

Crisp salads offer a welcome refreshment with spicy shrimp kebabs.

White cabbage and bacon salad

Mix strips of white cabbage with fried bacon, and diced red and green bell peppers. Mix with a dressing of vinegar, bacon fat, salt, black pepper and chives.

Cucumber and dill salad

Cut a cucumber in half, deseed, and slice. Mix with thin strips of shallots, sour cream, lemon juice, dill, salt, pepper, and sugar.

Bok choy and radish salad

Mix 1 bunch sliced radishes with strips of bok choy and diced, skinned tomatoes. Toss in a dressing of lemon juice, oil, salt, pepper, and parsley.

SHRIMP
with tomatoes and red win

Serves 4

12	jumbo shrimp, peeled
4 tbsp	olive oil
1	shallot, finely chopped
2	garlic cloves, crushed
1	tomato, peeled and diced
7 tbsp	bouillon
3½ tbsp	red wine
	Salt
	Cayenne
1 tbsp	brandy
3 tbsp	butter (ice cold)

Step by step

Wash the shrimp under running water and pat dry with paper towels.

Pour over the bouillon and red wine. Season with salt and cayenne, then add the brandy.

Fry in 1 tablespoon of oil for about 3 minutes, tossing thoroughly. Remove from the pan and set aside.

Reduce the mixture by one-third, then thicken with ice-cold butter flakes.

Add the rest of the oil to the pan, sweat the shallot and garlic, and add the diced tomatoes.

Add the fried shrimp to the sauce, heat through, and serve.

TOMATOES INFO

For many recipes you need **peeled tomatoes**. It would be far too troublesome and time-consuming to peel raw tomatoes with a knife, so simply plunge them into boiling water, and the skin will almost come off by itself.

Before doing so, you must cut out the stalks with a sharp knife

and make a cross in the skin on the opposite side. Then plunge the tomatoes into boiling water, either singly or in portions. As

soon as the split skin begins to roll back, remove the tomatoes and rinse in cold water. Pull the skin off with a small knife.

SEAFOOD

SALADS
for shrimp

Vegetable salads go well with the delicious briny taste of shrimp—take these three, for example:

Leek salad

Cut leeks into pieces 4 in. (10 cm) long and cook for 10 minutes in salt water. Remove, drain (reserving some of the water), and transfer to a serving dish. Mix together vinegar, salt, sugar, pepper, a little of the leek water, and chopped parsley, and pour over. Leave to cool, drizzle with oil, and sprinkle with chopped, hard-boiled egg.

Cauliflower salad

Cook cauliflower florets al dente and mix with chopped onion. Cover with the cauliflower cooking water. Add salt, pepper, dill, oil, vinegar, and sugar. Chill in the icebox for at least 2 hours and drain well before serving.

Avocado salad

Peel 2 avocados. Cut one in half, and drizzle with lemon juice. Chop the other and purée with lemon juice, herbes de Provence, and yogurt. Add sherry, and season with salt and pepper. Serve onion rings and tomatoes cut into eight with the sliced avocado and sauce.

SHRIMP
severa

The different names for shrimp, as noted on page 134, refer to the differences in size. No matter what name they are sold under, however, you can use these recipes to prepare them. On these two pages, you will find four variations on the theme of shrimp: one from India, one from the Far East, and two from

... with ginger, curry, and bananas

Sweat 2 finely chopped onions, 2 crushed garlic cloves, and 1 piece finely grated ginger in butter until transparent. Make a roux with 2 tablespoons flour and 2 tablespoons curry powder. Gradually add 2 cups (500 ml) vegetable bouillon and 1 cup (250 ml) light cream, and bring to a boil. Add 2 puréed bananas, season with salt, pepper, and lemon juice, and heat the previously cooked shrimp in the sauce for about 4 minutes.

... with coconut cream and sambal ulek

Mix together $^3/_4$ cup (185 ml) coconut cream, the grated rind of 1 lemon, 1 tablespoon lemon juice, 2 tablespoons soy sauce, and $^1/_2$ teaspoon sambal ulek. In a wok, fry 1 segmented onion in 1 tablespoon peanut oil until transparent. Add the shrimp, and stir fry for about 2 minutes. Add the coconut cream mixture and cook for a further 3 minutes over medium heat, until creamy.

variations

Europe. With them, you can either try one of the
fresh salads, or rice, polenta, or couscous.

SIDE DISHES
for shrimp

Serve with a very special rice—saffron rice—or
perhaps with a completely different accompaniment,
such as delicate couscous or tasty polenta.

Saffron rice
Sweat 1¼ cups (250 g) rice in butter, and add a few saffron
threads. Pour over bouillon, add salt, and simmer for about
20 minutes over low heat. Fluff with a fork to let the steam
escape, and mix in 2 tablespoons butter flakes.

... with shallots and crème fraîche
Fry the shrimp in 5 tablespoons peanut oil, then remove from
the pan. Brown 4 finely chopped shallots and 2 crushed garlic
cloves in the oil. Pour over 3 tablespoons brandy and season
with salt, pepper, and cayenne. Reduce a little. Add ½ cup
(125 ml) light cream and crème fraîche. Serve immediately with
the shrimp.

Couscous
Bring couscous to a boil with about 1½ times the quantity
of vegetable bouillon and a little salt. Allow to swell for a
few minutes—and it's ready.

... with sugar snap peas and asparagus
Fry the shrimp in 1 tablespoon butter, and remove from the
pan. Brown 7 oz (200 g) chopped sugar snap peas, 1 bunch
chopped scallions, two crushed garlic cloves, and generous 1 lb
(500 g) chopped green asparagus, in the pan. Drizzle with
lemon juice and season with salt. Pour over ⅔ cup (150 ml)
light cream and cook. Add the shrimp, and cook for 2 minutes.
Season with 1 teaspoon mustard, pepper, salt, and lemon juice.

Polenta
Bring vegetable bouillon to a boil with salt and a little
butter, then stir in cornmeal. Bring back to a boil, while
stirring continuously, allow to swell for 3 minutes, then
stir in grated Parmesan.

LOBSTER THERMIDOR
au gratin, with Parmesan

INFO

If you use a live **lobster**, select a big enough pan, as you must be able to slide the lobster smoothly into the water so it is completely covered. Slide it claws first into boiling water, cover, and cook for 10 minutes. If you want to prepare the lobster in a different way, take it out, otherwise continue cooking it in the same liquid.

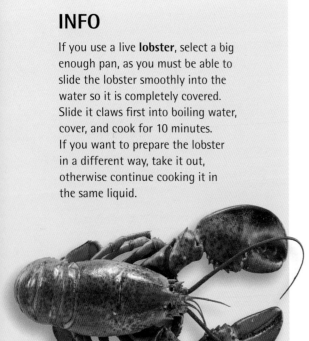

Serves 4

2	*live lobsters*
	Salt
	Pepper
1 cup (250 ml)	*fish bouillon*
1 tbsp	*white wine*
2	*shallots, finely chopped*
1 tbsp	*chervil, chopped*
1 tbsp	*tarragon, hacked*
2 tbsp	*butter*
2 tbsp	*flour*
1 tsp	*mustard powder*
	Nutmeg
1 cup (250 ml)	*milk*
5 tbsp	*Parmesan, freshly grated*

Step by step

Put the lobsters in a large pan of boiling water, boil for about 10 minutes, and remove.

Cut the lobsters in half lengthwise, remove the flesh from the shell and claws, and cut into small pieces. Season with salt and pepper.

Reduce the fish bouillon by one-half with the wine, shallots, and herbs. Then strain through a sieve.

Make a roux from butter and flour, then add the mustard powder and nutmeg. Stir in the strained stock with the milk and 2 tablespoons of grated Parmesan.

Arrange the lobster meat in the shell, and pour over the sauce. Sprinkle with the remaining Parmesan. Bake in the oven for 5 minutes at 400 °F/200 °C.

Side dish

With a special delicacy such as lobster it is best just to serve fresh **white bread**. This will allow the full flavor of the crustacean to be appreciated. But if you want the bread to be something special, too, then why not bake it yourself? Knead together scant 3 cups (400 g) wheat flour, 1¹/₂ tablespoons active dry yeast, ¹/₂ teaspoon sugar, and 1 cup (250 ml) water to make a dough. Leave to prove for 50 minutes. After 20 minutes, knead in 1¹/₂ teaspoons salt. On a floured surface, form the dough into 2 baguettes, and prove for a further 20 minutes. Bake for 45 minutes, with water in a pan on the oven shelf below.

Sauce

The basis of **mayonnaise** is an emulsion of egg yolk and oil, to which any other ingredients you like may be added—lemon juice, for example—but other flavoring ingredients such as spices, mustard, ketchup, and sherry are also suitable for mayonnaise. They can be made to go further by adding cream or, for a lighter version, with yogurt. Just try it out for yourself. With a whisk, beat egg yolk, salt, pepper, mustard, and vinegar together, while slowly adding olive oil in a thin stream to give a creamy mayonnaise.

SEAFOOD

SAUCES
for lobster

If the recipe does not provide for a sauce already, choose one of these suggestions to go with boiled or baked lobster:

Curry mayonnaise

Lightly brown finely chopped onions and garlic cloves in butter, add curry powder, and simmer for 2–3 minutes. Add a little water and simmer for a further 5 minutes. Cool, mix with mayonnaise and lime juice, and season with salt and pepper. Goes well with lobster with coconut milk, with mixed vegetables, and with leek and ginger.

Orange curaçao sauce

Lightly brown finely chopped onions in butter, add curaçao, fish bouillon, and orange juice, and reduce. Add more butter, and season with salt and pepper. Shortly before serving, warm orange segments in the sauce. Goes well with lobster with mixed vegetables, and with leek and ginger.

Madeira cream sauce

Sauté finely chopped shallots in butter until transparent. Stir in flour, then gradually add Madeira and cream, and simmer for about 4 minutes, stirring continuously. Beat together with egg yolk, and season with salt and cayenne. Goes well with lobster with mixed vegetables, and with leek and ginger.

LOBSTER
severa

Lobster can be prepared in various ways. If you want to boil it, it is best to use live ones, but only if you have no reservations about killing the creatures yourself. Otherwise, you can buy them ready boiled from the fishmonger or—easiest of all—buy them frozen. Incidentally, freshwater crayfish are also suitable for these recipes. The general rule for how

... with mixed vegetables and grapes

Mix generous $^3/_4$ cup (200 ml) fish bouillon with 4 tablespoons port and 2 tablespoons brandy, and reduce. Add 7 tablespoons (100 ml) light cream, and reduce again. Warm through 8 peeled grapes in the mixture. Blanch 2 diced carrots and 1 diced zucchini, 12 lima beans, and 12 sugar snap peas, and heat in butter. Add 1 diced tomato, and season with salt and pepper. Serve with boiled lobster tossed in butter.

... with leek and ginger

Sweat 1 piece ginger in strips and 3 onions in fine rings for 5 minutes in $3^1/_2$ tablespoons (50 g) butter, and season with salt and pepper. Add boiled lobster. Cover, and cook for about 8 minutes. Spread 1 leek in rings over the lobster, and cook for a further 4 minutes.

ariations

ong to cook them in salt water is as follows: a live obster weighing 1 lb (500 g) takes 12 minutes. For a further 1 lb (500 g) allow 10 minutes more, and for each extra 1 lb (500 g) of weight allow another 5 minutes. So, for a lobster weighing $2^{1}/_{4}$ lb (1 kg) that comes to 22 minutes' cooking time.

.. with lettuce and cocktail sauce

Cut boiled lobster into slices. Line 4 individual glass dishes with the leaves of 1 lettuce, and fill with lobster. Make a cocktail sauce from 7 tablespoons mayonnaise, 2 teaspoons tomato paste, 2 tablespoons brandy, 2 teaspoons lemon juice, 1 pinch powdered ginger, Tabasco® Sauce, paprika, and 3 tablespoons whisked light whipping cream, and spoon over the lobster. Serve with 3 tablespoons whisked light whipping cream and 1 slice each lime and truffle.

.. with coconut milk, bell pepper, and dates

Sweat 2 tablespoons curry paste and 1 chopped lemongrass stalk or 1 minute. Add pieces of lobster, fry for 3 minutes, and remove from the pan. Add 1 diced red bell pepper and brown briefly. Add cup (250 ml) coconut milk and 6 dried dates, and cook for 5 minutes. Add 1 tablespoon fish sauce, 2 teaspoons brown sugar, the grated rind of 1 lime, and the lobster pieces, and heat through.

SAUCES
for lobster

With saffron and tomatoes, white wine and lemon juice, or herbs—these sauces are also great with boiled lobster.

Herb, wine, and butter sauce

Bring butter briefly to a boil, and skim off the froth. Using a whisk, add chopped herbs such as parsley, chives, basil, and thyme, together with white wine. Goes well with lobster with coconut milk, with mixed vegetables, and with leek and ginger.

Saffron sauce with mushrooms and tomatoes

Sauté finely chopped shallots in butter. Briefly sweat thinly sliced mushrooms with them, add saffron, Noilly Prat and crème fraîche, and reduce a little. Thicken with butter flakes, and heat diced tomatoes in the sauce. Goes well with lobster with mixed vegetables, and with leek and ginger.

Sauce Choron

Beat together egg yolk, white wine, Worcestershire sauce, lemon juice, tomato paste, salt, and pepper. Beat to a cream over a pan of hot water. Melt butter, beat slowly into the sauce, and season again. Goes well with lobster with mixed vegetables, and with leek and ginger.

145

STUFFED SQUID
with Haloumi and onions

Serves 4

4	*squid (each about 7 oz/200 g), ready to cook*
2	*onions, finely chopped*
2 tbsp	*olive oil*
2	*garlic cloves, crushed*
1³/₄ oz (50 g)	*fresh brown bread, crumbled*
2 tsp	*parsley, chopped*
3¹/₂ oz (100 g)	*Haloumi, in cubes*
	Salt
	Pepper
1³/₄ lb (800 g)	*tomatoes, peeled and roughly chopped*
¹/₂ cup (125 ml)	*white wine*
1 tsp	*rosemary*

Step by step

Remove thin skin, head, ink sac, and fish bones from the squid. Cut off the tentacles, and chop small.

Heat a little olive oil, brown the squid on all sides, and remove from the pan.

Sweat 1 onion in oil until transparent. Mix with the tentacles, garlic, breadcrumbs, parsley, Haloumi, salt, and pepper.

Brown the remaining onion in the oil. Add the tomatoes and wine, and reduce over high heat.

Spoon the filling into the body, and close securely with toothpicks.

Add the squid, season with salt, pepper, and rosemary, and simmer for about 30 minutes.

CEPHALOPODS INFO

As with shrimp, there is a bewildering range of names for **edible cephalopods**. Three of the significant types are **squid**,

cuttlefish, and **octopus**. The latter, which can be anything from 18 in.–13 ft. (0.5–4 m) in length, are considerably bigger than most squid, which only grow to 2–8 in. (5–20 cm). When buying, remember that not all are as suitable for certain recipes, particularly stuffing, as

squid. Octopus have big, strong tentacles, a small, stocky body, and require a much longer cooking time. The cuttlefish is often not big enough for stuffing, plus the texture of its meat can be tough and chewy.

147

SALADS
for squid

A delicious salad makes an excellent complement to stuffed squid, and adds a refreshing note.

Feta salad with green bell pepper
Simply mix strips of green bell pepper and cucumber with onion rings and cubed Feta, and drizzle with a dressing of coarsely ground pepper, vinegar, and oil.

... with shrimp, Ricotta, and parsley
Mix 7 oz (200 g) diced Ricotta with chopped tentacles, 3 1/2 oz (100 g) cooked shrimp, 1/2 bunch finely chopped parsley, 2 crushed garlic cloves, salt, pepper, 1 teaspoon lemon juice, and possibly a little water, and spoon into the squid. Brush the squid with a little olive oil and cook in the oven for 20 minutes at 350 °F/180 °C, turning occasionally and brushing with oil.

Bell pepper salad with marinade
Cut red and green bell peppers into very thin strips, and slice an onion into rings. Make a dressing from lemon juice, salt, sugar, and oil, and fold into the vegetable mixture.

... with rice, basil, and raisins
Simmer the squid with its chopped tentacles for 10 minutes. Finely chop 1 bunch parsley, 2 sprigs basil, 2 garlic cloves, 1 tablespoon pine nuts, and 1 tablespoon raisins. Mix with 4 tablespoons boiled rice, 2 egg yolks, the grated rind of 1/2 lemon, salt, and pepper, spoon into the squid, and secure with soaked wooden toothpicks. Brush with oil, grill for 15 minutes, turn, brush with oil, and continue grilling until done.

STUFFED SQUID
s e v e r a l   v a r i a t i o n s

For stuffed squid, fill the tube, i.e. the body, with the finely chopped tentacles and other ingredients, and then braise or grill it.

... with ground meat, mushrooms, and capers

Mix together the chopped tentacles, 7 oz (200 g) ground meat, 3 tablespoons chopped parsley, 1³/₄ oz (50 g) diced mushrooms, 1 crushed garlic clove, ¹/₂ chopped onion, lemon rind, pepper, salt, and 1 egg. Spoon into the squid, then brown. Braise with ¹/₂ chopped onion and ¹/₄ cup (60 ml) each stock and white wine for about 30 minutes. Thicken the sauce, and flavor with parsley, 3 tablespoons capers, salt, and pepper.

... with anchovies and rosemary

Drizzle the squid tubes with the juice of 1 lemon. Mix chopped tentacles, 1 teaspoon rosemary, 1 bunch chopped parsley, 4 chopped anchovy fillets, 2 crushed garlic cloves, 3 tablespoons breadcrumbs, the grated rind of ¹/₂ lemon, salt, pepper, and 1 egg, spoon into the squid, and secure. Brush with olive oil, season with salt and pepper, sprinkle with rosemary, and grill for 20 minutes.

... with freshwater crayfish, Feta, and olives

Sweat 1 chopped red onion with 2 crushed garlic cloves, 3 tablespoons diced bacon, and 5¹/₂ oz (150 g) freshwater crayfish. Add ³/₄ cup (150 g) rice and 2 tablespoons tomato paste, and simmer. Add the chopped tentacles, 7 oz (200 g) Feta, 6 chopped olives, 3 chopped sun-dried tomatoes, 1 egg, and herbs, then spoon into the squid and secure. Brush with oil and grill for 15 minutes.

... with cured ham, chorizo, and white bread

Moisten 2 slices white bread in 1 egg yolk, and mix with 1 egg, salt, and pepper. Sauté 1 chopped onion and 1 crushed garlic clove, add the chopped tentacles, 1 slice chopped ham, 3¹/₂ oz (100 g) diced chorizo, parsley, and the bread, and spoon into the squid. Simmer for 30 minutes in ¹/₂ cup (125 ml) fish bouillon, with 1 shallot, 4 diced tomatoes, and 1 bay leaf.

SCAMPI
in t o m a t o s a u c e

Serves 4

1³/₄ lb (800 g)	scampi, ready to cook
4	onions, finely chopped
4 tbsp	oil
14 oz (400 g)	canned tomatoes
2 tbsp	tomato paste
	Salt
	Pepper
¹/₂ tsp	cumin
¹/₄ tsp	pimento
¹/₂ bunch	parsley, finely chopped
1	garlic clove, crushed

INFO

Small, edible lobsters (6–8 in./15–19 cm) are known as **scampi** in Italian; other names include Dublin Bay prawn; Danish lobster; and Florida lobsterette. They resemble small crayfish, but the fact that they are lobsters can be seen from their two large claws. An exception to this is the langoustine, which is found in the North Atlantic, and has no claws. The delicate flesh of these small lobster varieties, which are usually sold ready to cook, is found only in their tails. When prepared tails alone are sold, it is often under the name of scampi.

Step by step

Peel the scampi. To do this, twist the head and separate it from the body.

Remove the tail, cut the flesh lengthwise, and remove the black intestines.

Fry diced onions in oil over medium heat until golden brown. Add the canned tomatoes.

Mix the tomato paste with 1/2 cup (125 ml) of water and add to the tomatoes with the seasoning and spices. Reduce for 10 minutes, stirring continuously.

Add the chopped parsley and crushed garlic to the sauce. Season with salt.

Pour the sauce into an ovenproof dish, and spread the scampi over it. Cook for 10 minutes at 400 °F/200 °C, then for a further 20 minutes at 340 °F/175 °C.

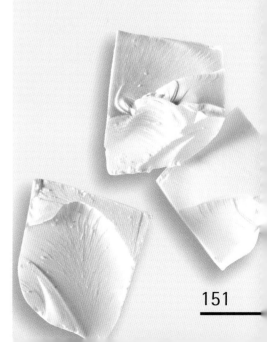

INFO

Feta, which originally comes from Greece, is a brine cheese. This means it is matured in brine, which gives it a strong, salty flavor of varying intensity. So be careful with the salt when using Feta. Incidentally, according to an EU regulation, only cheese produced in Greece from ewe's or goat's milk may be called Feta.

Salad

A Greek **Feta salad** goes perfectly with spicy tomato sauce. To make it, cut 1 large green bell pepper into strips, 1 large onion into rings, and 9 oz (250 g) Feta into small cubes. Slice 1 peeled cucumber. Mix together in a bowl with coarsely ground pepper, 1 tablespoon vinegar, and 3 tablespoons oil.

SALADS
for scampi

If you want something more filling and nourishing, try these three salads as an appetizer with scampi.

Olive and ewe's milk cheese salad with pine nuts

Mix cubes of Feta with diced tomatoes, pitted and sliced black olives, and scallion rings. Mix with a dressing of vinegar, oil, salt, and pepper. Stir in pine nuts.

Spinach and egg salad with croutons

Mix fresh young spinach leaves with chopped, hard-boiled eggs. Mix with a dressing of lemon juice, mustard, oil, salt, and pepper. Top with toasted croutons.

Fennel and mushroom salad

Mix strips of raw fennel with sliced mushrooms and black olives. Combine with a vinaigrette of vinegar, oil, salt, pepper, and saffron threads.

SCAMPI
severa

Fresh or frozen, scampi cook very quickly. Cook them for just a few minutes right at the end, or brown them briefly in advance. Whether you eat this protein-rich seafood plain, or serve it with one of the four sauces suggested below, is your decision. You can choose between red wine and onions, lobster stock and herbs, olives, capers, and tarragon,

... with red wine and onions

Sprinkle the scampi with salt, and fry without oil for 4 minutes; turn, and remove from the pan. Sweat 7 oz (200 g) sliced onions in oil until transparent. Bring to a boil with 1 tablespoon tomato paste, generous $^3/_4$ cup (200 ml) red wine, salt, and pepper. Add 11 oz (300 g) sliced tomatoes and 1 bunch chopped dill, cover, and simmer for 30 minutes. Then add the scampi and cook for a further 20 minutes.

... with olives, capers, and tarragon

Lightly brown the scampi and remove from the pan. Add 2 chopped onions to the pan. Strain 14 oz (400 g) canned tomatoes, and add to the pan, together with $3^1/_2$ oz (100 g) green olives and 1 tablespoon capers. Top up with 2 cup (500 ml) bouillon and generous $^3/_4$ cup (200 ml) white wine, and season with salt and pepper. Cook for about 30 minutes. Then add the scampi with 1 bunch chopped tarragon, bring to a boil, reduce the heat, and continue cooking for 20 minutes.

variations

and mixed vegetables with saffron. As an appetizer, we recommend one of these six delicious salads.

... with lobster stock, oregano, and thyme

Lightly brown the scampi in oil, then remove from the pan. Gently heat 2 tablespoons tomato paste in the pan. Add 2 chopped onions and sweat until transparent. Pour over 1 cup (250 ml) lobster stock. Add 14 oz (400 g) canned tomatoes, oregano, thyme, 2 bay leaves, salt, and pepper, and cook gently for 30 minutes. Then add the scampi and continue cooking for about 20 minutes.

.. with zucchini, eggplant, and saffron sauce

Dice 2 zucchini, 1 eggplant, and 4 scallions, and sauté in oil. Add 4 diced tomatoes, pour over 7 tablespoons (100 ml) wine and 1¹/₄ cups (300 ml) stock, and simmer for 25 minutes. Stir in 7 tablespoons (100 ml) light cream. Season with salt and pepper, and stir in ¹/₂ teaspoon saffron threads. Cook until smooth and creamy. Fry the scampi in a skillet in 3 tablespoons oil, add to the vegetables, and simmer for 10 minutes.

SALADS
for scampi

Simple salads are perfect both before, and with, scampi. You do not need anything else with them, except a fresh baguette.

Tomato salad

Mix together sliced tomatoes, finely chopped scallions, salt, and pepper, and leave to steep for at least 15 minutes. Give the salad a gentle stir before serving.

Iceberg lettuce

Hand shred iceberg lettuce leaves. For the dressing, mix chopped onion, oil, vinegar, sugar, salt, and pepper, and stir into the lettuce.

Lollo Biondo

Mix together olive oil, balsamic vinegar, medium-hot mustard, salt, pepper, lemon juice, and chile powder, flavor with chopped thyme, marjoram, and basil, and pour over shredded lettuce leaves.

153

ARBORIO RICE INFO

Arborio rice is a variety of rice that is particularly good for risotto. It is a medium-grain rice in the "superfino" category and named for the Piedmontese town of Arborio, around which the main cultivation areas are

located. Arborio has the biggest grains of all Italian rice varieties, and they are also rounder than others. All these qualities mean that the liquid becomes thick and creamy and the grains remain al dente.

PEAS INFO

Peas are sold fresh, dried, canned, or frozen. Fresh peas do not keep very long and quickly lose their flavor, so it is often preferable to go for the preserved kinds. Sugar snap peas are an especially

delicious type, available fresh in the spring, when the seeds have not yet developed. As you can tell from the name, they taste fresh and sugary.

Serves 4

1 lb (500 g)	*blue mussels*
9 oz (250 g)	*squid, cut into rings*
4¹/₂ oz (125 g)	*shrimp*
14 oz (400 g)	*fish fillets, roughly chopped*
4 tbsp	*oil*
	Salt, pepper
1 each	*green and yellow bell pepper, roughly chopped*
1	*onion, finely chopped*
2	*garlic cloves, crushed*
1¹/₄ cups (250 g)	*arborio rice*
1	*sachet saffron*
5¹/₂ oz (150 g)	*frozen peas*
	Juice of ¹/₂ lemon

Step by step

Wash the mussels (see page 123). Wash the squid, shrimp, and fish fillets, and pat dry.

Fry the fish, squid, and shrimp in 2 tablespoons of oil for 2–3 minutes, turning occasionally. Season with salt and pepper, and remove from the pan.

Brown the bell peppers and onions in the pan in 2 tablespoons of oil. Stir in the garlic and rice, and sweat briefly.

Dissolve the saffron and ¹/₂ teaspoon of salt in 4 cups (1 liter) boiling water, and add to the rice mixture. Bring back to a boil, while stirring continuously.

Add the fish and seafood. Reduce the heat and simmer for 20 minutes, adding the frozen peas for the last 5 minutes.

Leave the paella to stand for 5 minutes. Remove any unopened mussels, and season with salt, pepper, and lemon juice.

SEAFOOD PAELLA
with bell pepper and peas

SEAFOOD
several variations

You can buy mixed seafood frozen. The mixture usually consists of mussels, shrimp, and squid. Here are six variations:

... in red wine sauce with spaghetti

Cook 9 oz (250 g) spaghetti. While it is cooking, sweat 1 finely chopped onion in oil until transparent. Add 1 lb (500 g) frozen seafood and brown. Pour over $^1/_2$ cup (125 ml) red wine. When the sauce begins to boil, stir in 2 tablespoons crème fraîche, and thicken with a little flour if necessary. Season with oregano and salt. Serve the spaghetti in the sauce.

... with tuna on pizza

Roll out pizza dough and place on a greased baking sheet. Spread with tomato sauce made from 14 oz (400 g) canned tomatoes, 9 oz (250 g) thawed, frozen seafood, 1 can tuna, $3^1/_2$ oz (100 g) finely chopped shallots, and 2 crushed garlic cloves. Season with $^1/_2$ bunch chopped parsley, 3 tablespoons thyme, salt, and pepper. Top with $1^3/_4$ cups (200 g) Emmental and 4 tablespoons olive oil, and bake for 10–12 minutes at 430 °F/225 °C.

... in lemon sauce with macaroni

Cook 11 oz (300 g) macaroni. While it is cooking, brown 1 bunch chopped scallions in 2 tablespoons oil. Add 1 lb (500 g) frozen seafood, fry briefly, and season with salt and pepper. Bring 3 tablespoons white wine, 2 tablespoons lemon juice, 1 cup (250 ml) vegetable bouillon, and 7 tablespoons (100 ml) cream to a boil, and thicken. Stir in $^1/_2$ bunch finely chopped dill and season. Serve the macaroni in the sauce.

... with herbs as an appetizer

Thaw 1 lb (500 g) frozen seafood. Toss in a little olive oil and brown in a casserole. Continue cooking gently, gradually adding $^1/_2$ bunch thyme leaves, 4 sprigs rosemary, 2 sprigs lavender, $^1/_2$ bunch oregano, 1 sprig sage, 1 crushed garlic clove, the grated rind of 2 lemons, and $^1/_2$ bunch finely chopped parsley. Season with salt and pepper.

SALADS
for seafood

A fresh salad always goes well with seafood. Here are three suggestions:

Lamb's lettuce
Trim the roots of the lamb's lettuce. Dress with a marinade of vinegar, oil, salt, pepper, and sugar, and sprinkle with croutons.

Chicory salad
Cut the chicory leaves into $^1/_2$-in. (1-cm) wide strips. Serve in a dressing of vinegar, mustard, yogurt, sour cream, oil, salt, pepper, and ketchup.

Beet salad
Scatter freshly boiled, thinly sliced beet with cumin. Make a marinade of water, vinegar, salt, pepper, and sugar, and mix with the beet. Stir in oil when the beet has cooled.

. with vegetables and couscous
ring $3^1/_4$ cups (750 ml) bouillon to a boil, and crumble in 1 dried hile. Add 11 oz (300 g) each diced potatoes and carrot batons and mmer for 10 minutes. Add 11 oz (300 g) roughly chopped ucchini. After 5 minutes, add $1^3/_4$ lb (750 g) thawed seafood, and ok gently for 10 minutes. Stir in 9 oz (250 g) cooked couscous ong with 2 tablespoons raisins soaked in Marsala.

with a garlic and white wine vinegar marinade
aw $1^3/_4$ lb (750 g) frozen seafood. Cook for 2–3 minutes in t water, rinse in cold water, and drain thoroughly. Make a arinade from 6 tablespoons white wine vinegar, 5 tablespoons l, 2 crushed garlic cloves, 2 tablespoons each chopped parsley d granulated sugar, the juice of $^1/_2$ lemon, salt, and pepper, d pour over the seafood. Leave to steep in the icebox for at ast 30 minutes.

Index of recipes

Index of recipes